A CONTRIBUTIVE
SOCIETY

J. R. Bellerby, 1935

A CONTRIBUTIVE SOCIETY

By

J. R. BELLERBY

with additional papers

EDUCATION SERVICES
364 WOODSTOCK ROAD
OXFORD OX2 8AE
1988

Copyright © 1988 Education Services

First published 1931
Second edition 1988 with additions

A Contributive Society by J. R. Bellerby
ISBN 0–902812–02–5 hardback
0–902812–03–3 paperback

Printed in Great Britain by
Joshua Associates Ltd.
Oxford

CONTENTS

ACKNOWLEDGEMENTS

IN THE preparation of this volume, thanks are due to all members of Education Services for their advice and encouragement. Mrs Rosalind Bellerby has also helped greatly with historical records and recollections, and Mr Roger Sawtell with information on the Common Ownership Movement.

We gratefully acknowledge contributions from *The Economic Journal*, and the *Bulletin des anciens*; and thank also Miss Greta Horn and Mrs Joyce Morris for valuable assistance in typing and preparation of materials.

FOREWORD

BY
PROFESSOR SIR AUSTIN ROBINSON
Professer Emeritus of Economics,
Sidney Sussex College, Cambridge

I AM very glad that Bellerby's *A Contributive Society* is to be reprinted and made available for another generation. I knew Bellerby fifty years ago in Cambridge. He was very diferent from most of the other economists of those years. He was very much more interested than most of us in the more human issues. I regarded him as a very nice, rather saintly person. But it happened that we were both of us interested in many of the same things and I used to discuss them with him.

I find it interesting that the copy of the book in the Marshall Library in Cambridge, which I borrowed in order to revise my memories, is inscribed to Maynard Keynes by Bellerby himself and was passed to the librarian with others of Keynes's books after his death.

The book itself, as it seems to me, is well written in the simple English that in those days we were not ashamed to use as a means of communication. In that respect it is very different from most economic writing of today. It is written at the level of a layman writing for laymen, and not in the jargon of economics. And it deals with the broad problems of motivation and of economic ethics.

The remarkable thing about Bellerby's work is that results of it have survived. During the 1930s the thinking of people like Bellerby and like myself was very much more practical than it is today. If something was wrong, we did not organise a demonstration nor did we just sit back and do nothing. We tried to do something about it. Like Bellerby I was associated, largely under the inspiration of William Temple, then Archbishop of York, in one or two slightly similar schemes to help the unemployed form co-operatives and find employment for their time while doing something that raised their standards of life. But all the things with which I was associated died a few years later when the war brought full employment. In some curious way the institutions that Bellerby inspired have survived.

The thinking of the book is the complete antithesis of much currently dominant economic doctrine and the argument that the more selfish we are, the more we shall benefit the human race. It is built on the idea that one should concern oneself with the treatment of one's neighbours. That philosophy is by no means dead.

Bellerby will be remembered and should be remembered mainly for this book and its consequences.

INTRODUCTION
BY
J. O. JONES

FOR some years after the Second World War it appeared that the major problems of mankind, if not already solved, were at least capable of solution with the new tools and methods at hand. Advancing science and technology offered abundance of material goods and greatly enhanced services simultaneously with improved working conditions and reduction in human effort; whilst the "Keynesian revolution" in economic theory and practice[1] was believed to have removed for ever the persistant problems of widespread unemployment. But many of the advances in technology were found to be mixed blessings; and mass unemployment again became prevalent in the nineteen seventies and early eighties. Although higher national incomes in conjunction with sophisticated welfare schemes have reduced the pains of poverty in many industrial countries, the wastage of human potential and the frustration of those unable to obtain gainful employment and a dignified place in society became comparable to the situation of the nineteen twenties and thirties; whilst for those in employment relations between employers and employed showed little improvement. At present (1988) an encouraging revival in economic activity and employment, particularly in the U.K., restores faith in the operation of the market economy when

---

[1] Developing from *The General Theory of Employment, Interest and Money*, J. M. Keynes, 1936.

restrictions and interventions are reduced and material incentives are increased. However, whilst falling, the current U.K. unemployment level is yet $8 \cdot 2$ per cent or $2 \cdot 3$ millions, with almost one million unemployed for over a year.[2] This is still far above the 3 per cent indicated by Sir William Beveridge as necessary to allow for "change and freedom of movement from job to job."[3] And even in the most buoyant economy there is likely to remain a significant number who are unable to secure employment under fully competitive conditions. Yet most of these also have the need and ability to contribute to the society to which they belong. Regional and personal disparities in welfare remain and are possibly increasing. Harsh materialistic attitudes to life and work are felt by many to be prevalent, while crime and disorder indicate persistent failings in personal and social relationships. It is therefore very relevant to return to a significant publication of the inter-war period which both challenged orthodoxy and offered possible solutions to many problems then and now. It is also of value to trace the development in practice of some of the ideas put forward, for *A Contributive Society* is probably unique in being not only a theoretical construction but a practical scheme which was actually put into effect by the author and his friends. As stated by a reviewer in *The Economist* in 1931, "that any social reformer should in these days seriously propose to practise the social faith that he presents is sufficiently remarkable; that an economist of recognised standing should be afraid neither to practise nor to preach is an event that his colleagues cannot afford to ignore".

The author of *A Contributive Society*, John Rotherford (Jack) Bellerby was born in York in 1896. He had barely entered his

---

[2] July, 1988.

[3] *Full Employment in a Free Society*, Sir William Beveridge (later, Lord Beveridge), 1944, p. 21 and para. 169.

studies in 1914 at the University of Leeds when war broke out. He involved himself almost immediately and served with great merit on the Western Front throughout almost the whole period of the war, reaching the rank of major, and being awarded the Military Cross. His personal courage and inspiring leadership were widely recognised. He was severely wounded on the approaches to Passchendale in September 1917. Deep contemplation and prayer during convalescence led him to seek ways of improving economic and social conditions and enhancing industrial harmony. Following a distinguished academic performance at the University of Leeds, together with considerable sporting achievements despite having lost his right arm and suffered some eye damage on active service, Jack Bellerby quickly gained a post in the International Labour Office in Geneva. Experience in this Office, combined with study and travel in the United States, led to his consideration of what might be an ideal society and much of the text of *A Contributive Society* was formed in this period. It took final shape during the time of his Research Fellowship at Gonville and Caius College, Cambridge (1927–30).

Jack Bellerby's approach to economics was extremely positive. He saw the role of the economist as not only to describe and analyse, but also to prescribe; and having prescribed, to practise. Having determined what may be an ideal state, progress can be made towards the ideal both on a broad front, necessarily slowly, and by small groups deliberately associating and co-ordinating their action on the agreed principles so that by precept and example the movement might spread. Such a group, known as The Neighbours, was formed by Jack Bellerby in Cambridge. Central to its operation was the agreement of members to confine their personal expenditure to the average industrial wage (around three pounds per week at that time[4]), placing the remainder of their incomes in trust for agreed purposes in the light of *A Contributive Society* (Chapter 6). It is intriguing to imagine this practice in the context of an establishment hardly noted for its austerity. But knowing Jack Bellerby one can be sure that personal economies were achieved gracefully and without embarrassment to those as yet unconverted.

During this period (in 1929) Jack married the authoress, Frances Parker, who shared his ideals and became an enthusiastic member of The Neighbours. In a small booklet she encapsulated its essential spirit. "The Neighbours, consists of a small group . . . desirous of expressing concretely a variety of emotional, disturbing drives ('religions' if you like) . . . agreed . . . that about as good a way of doing this as any other is to be as contributive as possible and that obviously you cannot contribute what you have already spent on yourself. . . . Another advantage of being one of a group (is) the unfailing comfort of the feeling that if you *are* on a wild-goose chase you are in good company. Whilst if by any chance it turns out to be something more valuable than wild-geese, there will be others with you to share the excitement. . . . The group belief of The Neighbours is in the creative power of Beauty, Truth and Love; which belief inevitably leads to desire for expression in works."[5]

[4] For a single person. Married couples with one member working in the home were allowed £4, plus 10s. for each dependent child.

[5] *The Neighbours*, by M. E. Frances Bellerby, London. The Epworth Press. 12 pages, price Two Pence. See also *The Neighbours Ltd.*, p. 225 *et seq.* This paper was presented by Jack Bellerby to the Political Economy Club, Cambridge, at the request of the Chairman, J. M. Keynes. Sadly, no record can be traced of the ensuing discussion, or of Keynes' summing up. A stimulating description of the activities of Keynes' Political Economy Club is given by Sir Roy Harrod in *The Life of John Maynard Keynes*, Macmillan, 1951, pages 150–2 and 327–30. These pages include an account of the Club by Professor Sir Austin Robinson, taken from *The Economic Journal*, March, 1947.

But, it is fair to ask, is this more than an interesting, valiant, but quixotic episode, one further attempt to delineate a Utopia inevitably to be overwhelmed in the daily grind for survival and advantage? What happened to The Neighbours? It appeared that no additional group copied this example on identical lines, and the original Neighbours inevitably passed away. However, at least two threads of continuity can be traced. Much of the accumulated surplus income of The Neighbours was invested in a charitable trust and association known as Education Services. Jack Bellerby himself was a most active member of the Association until his death in 1977, and continuity has been maintained by a succession of new members. Present members of Education Services (eleven in number at the time of writing), are not bound by the rather strict and formal rules of The Neighbours, and the extent of their involvement in the Association varies widely. However, the spirit of contribution remains central and although their individual incomes and estates may differ and are entirely their private concerns, it would not be surprising to find that in fact their personal expenditures were generally within the bounds of the average industrial wage, and the concept of trusteeship was dominant in relation to their property.[6] Certainly their resources are broadly disposed. Involvement of present members extends widely and deeply into the fields of accountancy, agriculture, animal welfare, architecture, conservation, co-operation, development, economics, education, geography, human ecology, industrial relations, jurisdiction, peace studies, publication, and town and country planning. Over the years Education Services has been able to assist and collaborate with a wide number of students, authors and projects. Often help has been provided at highly critical stages in careers and project development. In keeping with the spirit

[6] cf. *A Contributive Society*, page 59.

of *A Contributive Society* priority is given to projects in which members themselves are involved. Secondly, help is given to projects and individuals known and recommended by members. Finally, when resources permit, grants are awarded in response to suitable direct applications without member contact. Efforts are made to establish and maintain links with projects and individuals, and to offer support and encouragement beyond the giving of financial help. [*See* Appendix I][7]

The second strong thread of continuity lies in the linking with a movement which began later and quite independently, but with many similarities. In 1951, a highly successful entrepreneur and manufacturer within the chemical industry, Ernest Bader, who had developed a private company, Scott Bader Ltd., concluded that the ownership and management of the company which he had built up should be vested in all those who worked within it; and that the principle of common ownership so developed provided a solution for many of the current problems of industrial organisation, income distribution and social responsibility. So began the modern Industrial Common Ownership Movement (ICOM)[8] and although there are similarities with older forms of co-operation, the common ownership movement includes a number of distinctive features. *A Contributive Society* was brought to Ernest Bader's attention in 1971 by a friend of Jack Bellerby's, the eminent economic statistician, Caradog Jones. Ernest was enraptured by this conceptual organisation which corresponded closely to so many of his own thoughts and ideals, and the anticipation of the benefits and problems of an industrial organisation in which traditional divisions between ownership, management

---

[7] The appended list of assisted publications and projects over recent years gives a partial indication of the range of involvement.

[8] The life and work of Ernest Bader are well recorded by Susanna Hoe in *The Man Who Gave His Company Away*, Heinemann, 1978.

and labour are swept away.[9] And may not unemployment be overcome by mutual service and sharing?[10] A meeting was quickly arranged at Jack and Rosalind Bellerby's home in Oxford. Ernest and his wife Dora (nee Scott) were accompanied by Fred H. Blum, who had recently completed a study of the Scott Bader Commonwealth,[11] and Roger Sawtell, then Managing Director of a new common ownership company, Trylon Ltd. The writer of this introduction was also present and felt the meeting charged with emotion and potential in the coming together of the two contrasting yet mutually sympathetic personalities, Jack's logical systematic analysis so nicely balancing and complementing Ernest's boisterous instinctive convictions and practical achievements. A close association between Education Services and the common ownership movement has developed steadily from this meeting; Roger Sawtell's key role has continued to expand and he has also become a Trustee and Member of Council of Education Services. There are now over 1,000 common ownership enterprises and this number is steadily increasing. In Roger Sawtell's words, each is "no more and no less than a group of people who wish to have control over the work they do and over the disposal of any surplus arising from it".[12] Normally provision is made by common ownership companies to use part of their surplus for the benefit of the wider community. It is interesting to consider how closely this corresponds to the pattern of The Neighbours, and whether these enterprises may be the "outposts" which Jack Bellerby had in mind.[13] Having left Trylon as a fully viable business and after

[9] cf. *A Contributive Society*, pp. 209–10. Industrial Relations.

[10] cf. *A Contributive Society*, p. 162.

[11] Fred H. Blum, *Work and Community: The Scott Bader Commonwealth and the Quest for a New Social Order.* Routledge and Kegan Paul, 1968.

[12] Roger Sawtell, Contribution to Annual Report, Education Services, 1984.   [13] *A Contributive Society*, Introduction, pp. vii–xiii.

spending some time shepherding through Parliament enabling
legislation which became the Industrial Common Ownership
Act 1976, Roger Sawtell returned to the grassroots to launch
and manage a new common ownership enterprise, Daily Bread
Co-operative Ltd. in Northampton—a whole-food warehouse
and packing business. This is a working group now of eighteen
people, and an annual turnover of more than £500,000.[14]
Alongside this venture, a shared housing community has
developed. Appropriately, in sympathy with Jack Bellerby's
original group, this new community has adopted the name of
The Neighbours. At present it is made up of four families in
five adjacent terrace houses in Northampton. Each family lives
separately but the houses are inter-connected so that these
Neighbours share various areas and possessions, such as the
garden, in which the boundary fences have been removed to
create a large space, a meeting room, spare bedrooms,
washing machine, and freezer. They meet regularly to eat
together, discuss, support each other, and worship together
as a group of Christians. An emerging objective of this shared
housing project is to provide some supportive accommodation
for people recovering from mental illness, who often have
nowhere to go after leaving psychiatric hospital and are striving to live in open society. It is possible that this form of
mutual enhancement and support will become a further mani-
festation of *A Contributive Society*.

Following the writing of *A Contributive Society*, and his
Research Fellowship at Caius College, Jack Bellerby's aca-
demic career continued as Brunner Professor of Economic
Science at Liverpool University, teaching being combined with

---

[14] It is considered that there is scope in the U.K. for 50 more similar co-
operatives, creating about 700 jobs for a total initial capital of less than £1
million. R. Sawtell, *Blueprint for 50 Cooperatives*, Cooperative Development
Agency, 1986. .

the wardenship of a students' hostel. It was at Liverpool where the link was established with Caradog Jones, Reader in Social Statistics. This led to collaboration in studies in employment[15] and later to Jack's joining Caradog's group: The Fellowship of the Spirit. Other of Jack's publications during this period include such diverse items as *Coal Mining: A European Remedy*, *Wages Policy and the Gold Standard*, and *Industrial Survey of Merseyside* (joint author). His 1932 address to the British Association for the Advancement of Science was reprinted in 1964 in *Essays in the Economics of Socialism and Capitalism*. By this time, Jack's early plea for the raising of public expenditure during periods of depression had become the new orthodoxy.

However, academic life, even in this abundance, did not seem to offer to Jack Bellerby sufficient opportunity to make his maximum contribution to society at a time when the dangers of another world war were increasing, and when he believed that the government's monetary and banking policies were quite wrong. Thus Jack entered actively into political life, joining the Labour Party and standing first, unsuccessfully, for Newark, and then in 1932 for Cambridgeshire. To respond fully to this call he felt compelled to resign his Chair at Liverpool. In his campaigning, he aimed at world peace through the enforcement of a Charter of Nations by an International Police Force under the League of Nations, and at full employment and prosperity through reform of monetary policy, banking and investment. Throughout the campaign his deep spirituality and Christian commitment became apparent. But despite an impressive performance, he failed to gain election.

This strenuous period had taken a toll of Jack's energies. Also his wife, Frances, was suffering severe ill-health, which

---

[15] *Full Employment and State Control*, by D. Caradog Jones, 1945, includes a contribution by J. R. Bellerby.

caused Jack great anxiety. Following the election campaign, they spent much time together, quietly, in the South of England and the West Country; but, sadly, their relationship was becoming strained. The outbreak of war in 1939 galvanised Jack's life anew, drawing him back into more active participation in national life; but Frances' own creative work was more successful in the relative isolation of the countryside. Jack returned briefly to Cambridge, then proceeded to the University of Glasgow where he held the Leverhulme Research Fellowship from 1940 to 1943. Here, together with study of current problems, he was able to cast his mind ahead to the challenges to come. Thus much of his concern was with the preparation of a book, *Economic Reconstruction: A Study of Post-War Problems.* Dominant in his thoughts was the principle that the essential purpose of reconstruction must be the "full employment of any citizen who seeks work." For four years from 1943 Jack Bellerby worked in the Ministry of Food on the vital task of ensuring adequate national food supplies, and also on post-war reconstruction and planning. During this time Jack maintained contact with Frances, travelling frequently to spend time with her in Cornwall. However, they parted formally in 1948, and their marriage was finally dissolved.

Jack's newly developed interest in food and agriculture in relation to overall employment and economic development led to his last academic appointment as University Demonstrator at the Oxford Institute for Research in Agricultural Economics, which was directed at that time by the eminent economist, Colin Clark. Already influenced and challenged by much of Colin's writings, particularly *The Conditions of Economic Progress*, Jack proceeded to make a significant contribution within this new setting in his definitive work, *Agriculture and Industry: Relative Income*, together with a succession of studies on contemporary issues in agricultural economics. [Published in *The Farm Economist*, see Appendix II.]

In 1961 Jack retired from formal academic employment. Also in that year he married Rosalind James, who had administered the Oxford Institute for Research in Agricultural Economics since its early days under the direction of C. S. Orwin. In this extremely fruitful partnership, Jack's efforts expanded into many fields, including animal welfare, with the publication of *Farm Animal Welfare and World Food* (evidence tendered to the Committee of Enquiry on Intensive Livestock Husbandry), and *Factory Farming*. Work continued on economic policy and co-operative endeavours; new interests developed in human ecology; and progressively more thought was given to the fundamental problems of life and the workings of the Holy Spirit. In this latter quest he found great joy and peace which he strove to express in conversation and writing to the time of his death.

In his economics work Jack Bellerby was among the first of John Maynard Keynes' colleagues to appreciate the significance of Keynesian doctrine relating to the management of the economy, and the deliberate stimulation of demand through public investment together with the "multiplier" to encourage and maintain employment. During the 1960s and 1970s this became the "conventional wisdom"; but just as the Classical Economics theories failed to explain or offer remedies for the economic depression and chronic unemployment of the 1930s, so Keynesian policies also began to lose their effectiveness. "Stop–Go" and "stagflation" dominated the economy whilst unemployment mounted despite massive public spending. Having been associated with Keynes, Jack agreed in conversation with the present writer that Keynes would have deplored many of the policies then continued in his name, and would have been the first to recognise that changing situations call for changing measures. The neccessary flexibility was certainly found in Jack Bellerby's thoughts. By the early 1970s he had become increasingly anxious and disturbed about inflation with its destruction of the value of money, and about the extremely adverse balance of payments of the U.K. He was convinced that monetary control and discipline were essential and should then receive priority in government policy. This was evident in his booklet, *Britain in Debt?*, which was circulated amongst a group of colleagues and policymakers.

As indicated by the appended list of publications [Appendix II], much of Jack Bellerby's writing dealt, at a high level of professional competence, with the problems of their time. *A Contributive Society* appears on a different level as a work of imagination and vision yet with a remarkable practical aspect, with a relevance well beyond its contemporary setting.

The accompanying essay by Alan Harrison indicates the striking modernity and present relevance of much of Jack Bellerby's writing, and draws valuable comparisons and contrasts with the writings of two modern socio-economists, Fred Hirsch and John Rawls. This comparative study places *A Contributive Society* in its appropriate academic setting, and by combining the thoughts of three outstanding authors, creates a new synthesis in economic and social theory.

Following Alan Harrison's essay *A Contributive Society* has been reproduced as originally written and printed. Some theories and practices mentioned, particularly in education, may now be largely superceded; but their interest and importance remain as an indication of the intellectual and social context of the inter-war period when radical new ideas were being formed and applied. Together with its central ideas which remain strikingly relevant, the complete book is part of an influential tradition in British intellectual life. An earlier paper, *The Neighbours Limited*, which is also included, further illuminates this period and throws additional light on *A Contributive Society*. The comprehensive review by P. A. Stone, from *The Economic Journal*, provides valuable commentary and appraisal, again in the context of the inter-war period. By a remarkable coincidence, the memoir by Archie Evans of the International Labour Office appeared in *Bulletin de anciens* while the present book was being prepared for press. It is most pleasing that this new edition of *A Contributive Society* should begin and end with recollections and commendations from colleagues of those Cambridge days.

Before allowing the text once again to speak for itself, it should perhaps be mentioned that Jack Bellerby was quite aware that many of his points were controversial, and that some of his proposals were not always easy to carry through. This is fully reflected in a later work, *The Conflict of Values*.[16] Difficulties of applying rigid and precise limits on personal expenditure within marriage and during illness are admitted (perhaps from experience). Also the fact is faced that different people may require differing conditions involving varying expenditure in order to maximise their respective contributions. But generally it may be considered that his later self-criticism was unduly severe, and that the essence of *A Contributive Society* remains unscathed both as a challenge and as a way forward. Members of Education Services offer the new presentation in this belief; and also as a tribute to a much loved colleague, and a remarkable man.

---

[16] *The Conflict of Values*, J. R. Bellerby, Education Services, 1933.

A CONTRIBUTIVE SOCIETY

By

J. R. BELLERBY

EDUCATION SERVICES
28 COMMERCIAL ST.
LONDON, E.1
1931

ACKNOWLEDGMENTS

THE present work has been written during breaks in other activity over a period of about three years, and in consequence shows the considerable changes of confidence felt during that time. At present, confidence is receding, at least in the possibility of discovering remedies that are simple. The feeling grows that, if in any sphere there exists a remedy, this is discernible as a rule only as some compromise between two aims, either of which, if followed to its extreme, would become incompatible with the other. A simple solution may always be shown if one aim is thrown into relief. But the aim, thus isolated, is found in the end to be empty. Probably much of the work here may be criticised on such grounds; and it is hoped that some redress may be made later through the issue of a further brief study, written in criticism of this and expressing the views of others who would help. The present work would have been even less satisfactory but for suggestions by Miss D. C. Rutter which have led to much revision, and some valued notes by Mr. M. R. Stack. A permanent debt for aid given at much personal cost must be expressed to the members of a small group without, if possible, laying on them any of the findings; both in America and in this country there have been friends whose willingness to experiment along the lines of this book has been a keen encouragement and is perhaps the only justification for its being published. To a creditor of long standing, Mr. J. M. Keynes, I am in debt for criticisms, not so far expressed here, which seem to touch the root of the thesis.

INTRODUCTION

THERE appear to be two chief difficulties confronting those who are anxious to see some change in the "economic system." The first is that of visualising a system which would in all ways reflect or express their ideal; the second is that of determining what steps may be taken, here and now, towards the attainment of the ideal. The chief purpose in this pamphlet is to join forces with those who are striving with these two problems.

There seems no escape, in the first place, for any who wish to be rational in their approach to economic reform, from attempting to determine what would be the "ideal." This is in no sense sentimentalism. It is simply a logical requirement. Some vision of the ideal economic system is necessary to give, as it were, "a point to march on" for those moving forward in the present. Moreover, some clear objective must be seen if the various elements of the general scheme of progress are to be coherent. The "ideal" is the focal point which ensures the convergence of all efforts.

To see the desired ultimate condition, and to describe it, does not imply, however, that the condition is regarded as immediately attainable. There is no necessity, even, that the state of perfection as conceived should be attainable at any future time. All that is needed is that it should be such as to permit the assertion : " The *more nearly* this state is approached, the more fully will human purpose be achieved."

Thus, however difficult the discussion of an economic Utopia may be, it must be taken up as a matter of course in any discussion of economic reconstruction. Some attempt must be made to visualise the type of economic system which would enable man to reach his highest human stature.

The difficulty of this problem may not, perhaps, be so great as appears at the outset; and, provided that a certain initial point of view is acceptable, the task it presents would seem by no means insuperable. The nature of the ideal economic system may be established by a clear and consistent approach if a certain assumption may be made concerning the character of the individuals composing the system. This assumption involves, however, some developing.

Its basis is broadly this : The character of the system and the character of the people composing it are inseparable. Given a people of a certain type and quality, the nature of the system they will erect will follow; it will exactly reflect the character of the people. And the system, once established, will tend to *re*produce men of the same type as those who

founded it. There is a constant action and inter-
action between the character of the system and the
character of the individuals working in it.

Of the two, however, it is the individual who is the
more important for consideration. In the first place,
he is the only real entity. He is the only thing with
feeling, with consciousness, and with ultimate value.
The State may be regarded perhaps as an organism,
as a thing capable of harmony or disharmony. But it
cannot " feel." It has no real being apart from the
members who compose it. The individual alone
senses the throb of emotion, and it is he alone who
truly counts. Thus, the essential test of any economic
system must be the type of individual it tends to
reproduce. Plato's Republic, for instance, or Marxian
Communism, or any form of social constitution, must
stand or fall according to the character of the citizen
implied.

Moreover, the individual may be regarded as the
more important for consideration, since upon him the
responsibility for the nature of the system ultimately
rests. In essence, the economic system is nothing
else than the associated conduct of all the members;
and according to the character of the members, so
will be their conduct. Thus an inferior people, if
self-governing, will set up an inferior economic system.
And a more perfected people will set up a more nearly
perfect economic system. If it were possible to
imagine a community of individuals who have arrived

at complete perfection, the economic system they would erect would be the ideal.

This, then, gives the necessary clue for discovering the nature of the ideal economic system : Assume the existence of a community of individuals who satisfy the most exacting definition of social merit, and then ask the question : How would they act? What principles would they set up to govern their economic conduct?

This approach, which will be the one attempted here, meets at the outset one difficulty : There can be no perfect representative of the human race as a whole. There may be a perfect teacher, or a perfect captain of industry, or a perfect second-in-command, or a perfect home-maker; but there can be no one character which embraces all types of perfection. Hence, if it is impossible to conceive of a single representative ideal citizen, it must be equally impossible to imagine a whole community of ideal citizens, and therefore the proposed method must break down at the outset.

This difficulty may be escaped, however, if attention is confined exclusively to economic life. For, in the discussion of economic affairs, the concern lies solely with the attitude of individuals to the production and consumption of goods; and the attitude of the socially perfect individual to these things may be defined, it seems, in a manner which should raise little question. Perfection in this respect, expressed in economic terms, would consist in " the desire to make the maximum contribution to communal consumption." In other words, the socially perfect individual would be distinguished by his anxiety to produce all he could, in order that the amount available for the whole body of the community should be the greatest. His production might not necessarily be material goods; but in whatever ways he was employed, his aim would be to render the fullest service of which he was capable to society as a whole.

This, then, is the basic assumption needed : If there existed a community of men whose accepted aim was to contribute their maximum to the consumption of the entire group, the type of economic system they would set up would be the ideal. And, on this assumption, the way to determine the nature of the ideal system would be simply to postulate the existence of such a community and then consider how, precisely, they would act.

It will be found, as will be seen later in Chapter VI, that various of the more important features of the ultimate economic state can be deduced with certainty from this initial assumption. Sufficient can at least be discovered of the desired state to yield significant directives for the effort of reconstruction in the present.

It is upon the second main problem, however, that the discussion here will chiefly range—namely, the problem : How far is it possible, immediately, to press forward towards the ideal? There are many who can never be content merely to see a distant and intangible vision of perfection and then leave it as a factor in general education or as a vague directive for personal conduct. Their need is rather for some immediate and fairly drastic move : some forward plunge which will mark a positive and visible gain of principle.

For various reasons on which there will be occasion to reflect later, the possibility of moving society forward *on its entire front* is inevitably very limited. Undoubtedly, certain methods of social reconstruction, the legislative, and the educational, do make for the greatest possible width of advance; but the advance is correspondingly narrow in depth; and this "gradualness" of forward movement is far from · giving satisfaction to those who wish in their own time to realise some practical expression of their social pattern.

There is, however, a second possible way of advance. It consists in the establishment of small pockets of society, groups which are bent on making personal experiment towards some social model. Such groups might begin merely as reconnaissance posts, attempting by trial and error to establish such rules of personal and business conduct as would bring them nearer their accepted pattern. But whereas each might thus at first regard itself as only an outpost, the hope would be that, as it became more firmly grounded and succeeded in evolving rules at once satisfying and widely practicable, it might expand. With the consolidation of each local group, and the growth of others, a steady penetration of the main body of society might be realised, the development of social principle being thereby quickened.

There appears to be no conflict between these two methods. Indeed, were the second " outpost " method to prove successful, it would help the other, in that it would show in concrete form certain objectives towards which industry's " wide-front " progress might be guided. The concern throughout these pages will, however, rest almost exclusively with the course consisting of the setting up of " outposts."

This method, involving as it does some definite attempt on the part of those with social theories to test them in personal practice, has received surprisingly little attention. Possibly the failure may be due to a certain feeling that it would be presumptuous to form any group which by virtue of its accepted aims must appear to regard itself as a caste apart from, and in advance of the rest of society. But surely this is not fair ground for scruple. In essence the aim of such a group would be, merely, to establish a new goal, a system which to them seemed more sociable. The one slight point of severance between them and others would be that they had seen different values. This should certainly not appear to imply an arrogation of superiority, since there is no means of proof that one set of values is of higher essence or reality than another. Indeed, it might with some force be shown that the greatest values possible are those found within the family or small intensive circle, and that to desert these in favour of some concern for "systems" is to exchange the substance for the shadow. It might be held, moreover, that those who seek these abstract outer values show rather a poverty of emotion than warmth, and are of inferior mettle.

If, as would be so, the seekers themselves felt that they had perceived something richer, they would give chase : and no doubt this would involve them in new ways of action. They would need to be little trammelled by convention, and would need the gift of seeing life not too seriously and not too lightly; but apart from this, one feels, there should be no difference between this group, as they pursued their discovery, and any others. They would be simply spreading out along lines which to them meant more robust self-realisation.

Thus for the purpose of this study it will be convenient throughout to make the assumption that there exists a group envisaging the type of problem in mind here. It will be assumed that there has been formed a comity of friends anxious to experiment personally in economic matters; and that they intend to keep close company, to give mutual aid and to maintain some unity of method. On these assumptions the attempt will be made to treat the various chief problems which such a movement would encounter in its approach to the distantly conceived state. Many questions, academic, philosophic, and educational, would arise and would have to be solved before an accepted basis could be reached for the joint experiment; and it is towards the solution of these questions that the chapters below are mainly turned.

The first problem would evidently be that of making a thorough analysis of the existing economic system. Since the intention of the new society would be to grow up within the established system, maintaining connection with it at all possible points, using the same instruments, and adopting as many of its customs as seemed compatible with progress towards the contemplated future pattern, it would need to scrutinise carefully the existing system, to determine which parts of it should be abandoned and which retained. This task of analysis is considered in the four ensuing chapters, where attention is given in turn to : the defining and describing of the present economic system; the consideration of its origins and the causes of its having assumed its present form; the examination of what is good and what is bad in the present system; and finally, a more detailed discussion of the most important feature, the basic motive of industry.

Then, as regards the Society's problems of construction, the first would be those relating to general education. The members would need to devise a system of early training and adolescent education capable of eliminating the defects felt in their own outlook, and likely to produce the type of personality required for the further extension of their society. Some suggestions as to the plan on which such a system might be developed are made in Chapter V.

In Chapter VI an outline is given of the possible stages of growth of the society itself. Initially, it is shown as a somewhat casual fellowship, prospecting on the basis of fairly elastic principles. The bond connecting the members would be essentially personal, and would be founded on little more than the grip of an idea. They would, however, from the outset proceed to evolve a code of rules for governing their behaviour as producers and consumers. These rules might be confined to a statement of broad principle at first; more detailed applications and interpretations would follow later. From these beginnings, the possible liens of extension and consolidation of the society are traced forward, the directive for its evolution being given throughout by the concept held of the ideal economic state. Finally, after the traversing of the various stages of its growth, a distant and, as to certain points, more speculative position is shown in which the society might emerge as an independent organism, comprehensive enough to be termed an " economic system."

CONTENTS

A CONTRIBUTIVE SOCIETY

CHAPTER I

THE ECONOMIC SYSTEM

THE extreme difficulty of giving a compact and at
the same time fairly comprehensive picture of the
economic system may justify, perhaps, the use of a
certain device of presentation. The economic system
may be described by means of an analogy with any
machine. In reality, although human, the system is
in the fullest sense a machine, in that it produces
goods by processes that are controlled, regular, and
almost mechanically systematic.

The analogy may be pressed further to several
detailed points. In the first place, every factory
machine is driven by an appropriate *motive power*.
The economic system is similarly driven : by human
motive. Secondly, every factory machine has certain
containers or *controls* to direct the power into its
requisite channels, and to prevent false escapes. The
human motive driving the economic system is likewise
controlled : through the medium of an elaborate
scheme of law. The whole legal system is, in fact, a

B

device for keeping men's motives within bounds and allowing them no outlet except through constructive channels. Finally, a factory machine has *behaviour*. It passes through certain regular motions, stereotyped, meticulously repeated, in the process of producing the goods for which it has been designed. In the case of the economic system, behaviour exists of the same almost mechanistic kind; in the production of goods, men follow certain regular habits, and perform actions daily in ways which are law-governed, almost unchangingly repeated, and in some cases inevitable.

If such an analogy has been used here, its purpose is not merely to simplify description in this chapter; but to indicate something which is fundamental: the existence of an organic connection between all the parts of the economic system. The motive underlying industry is the first and chief consideration. Then, according to the nature of the motive, so must be the controls. The legal system must provide controls specially adapted to prevent men's motives from finding destructive outlets; and different motives will involve different controls. Further, as will be seen later, almost all the " behaviour " of the system —its outward business habits—depends upon the character of the underlying motive which prompts action, and upon the legal system, which governs not only the motive, but also the ways in which it finds expression.

It is thus necessary to look upon the economic system not only as a thing of three major parts—motive, controls, behaviour—but also as a thing comprising parts most fully adjusted to one another at every point. The relation between them is as close, for instance, as the flow of water, the artificial course, and the electric current from a hydraulic power-station.

Moreover, into these three divisions, motive, controls, and behaviour, every feature of the system without exception can be classified. It is an all-comprising scheme. Hence, the purpose in this chapter will be to enumerate the most significant of the features, linking them together, and showing their connection, under these three main groups.

The Motive of Industry.

If, as has just been said, the basic driving power of industry is to be found in men's incentives, the task of discovering the character of this power is one primarily of psychology. The question is to be asked : What forces actuate men ? What are the inner constraints keeping them individually to the wheel and thus giving power to the industrial machine as a whole ?

A moment's thought shows that the motives involved are not one, but many. A man may strive because he is interested in self or interested in others; because he is anxious to acquire or anxious to serve.

And between these extremes there is an infinite range of shades of motive. Moreover, an added complication is that in any given person there may be a combination of influences working. All men must begin by attending to their physical needs; and their first motive to work will inevitably be to secure the materials of subsistence; but when this stage is past there may arise a wide variety of motives in which self-interest gradually merges into other-interest : the desire for intellectual development; the desire to maintain a family and ensure its well-being; the desire to stand high in the affection and esteem of one's fellows; and the desire to add something to the common stream.

In spite of the great diversity of motives which exist, there is no escape from the necessity of finding their " average " for use as the basis of discussion whenever any economic or social topic is being treated. All works on general economic principles have to meet this problem at the outset and ascribe to man some average incentive as the main determinant of his actions. The incentive usually selected as being widely representative is that of " enlightened self-interest." It is this motive which is attributed to the " economic man," when, in analysis, such a man is required to act as basis of deduction. Thus, although " enlightened self-interest " may be a somewhat indefinite term, the fact that it has been chosen by most economists as representing the average influence at work is significant, inasmuch as it points to a widely held belief that the motive on which industrial activity *now* primarily depends is man's keenness in pursuit of interests centring on himself.

If this belief concerning the motive of industry is well-founded—a matter which must be considered later—it is of cardinal importance for any study of the economic system. For there is this special property attaching to the motive : it pervades the entire system. It permeates the system as its life force, being the spring of action at all points. Once mentioned, this must seem obvious; for there can be no business habit, nor a single act in industry, which is not done or followed " with a motive."

This consideration will have the utmost importance at a later stage when the sound and the unsound are being distinguished in the existing system. For it is frequently the motive behind the business act, rather than the act itself, which determines whether it does or does not please.

For some reason, not readily understood, the question of the underlying driving force of industry appears to have been largely omitted from the sphere of " economics." The tendency has been to regard this subject as falling within the scope of ethics, and because it has thus been possible to give it a separate label, it has ordinarily been excluded from other discussions labelled " economics." The tendency cannot, it seems, persist; sooner or later the

economist or social leader who recommends new
economic mechanism without reference to the power
available to drive it will come to be judged as, say,
an engineer who builds machinery for which no
suitable form of power can be found. The question
of motive would seem inseparable from that of
structure; for, since the motive of industry provides
its sole source of energy, to neglect this in any project
for industrial change would be to neglect the essential.

Legal and other Controls.

The motive of industry would not always necessarily find expression in ways that are constructive,
were it not definitely confined and directed into
fruitful channels by some external control. As in
the case of any other explosive force, it would tend to
find an outlet along the line of least resistance. Thus,
in the not far distant past, the motive of self-interest
was sufficiently strong and sufficiently uncontrolled
to gain direct expression in brigandage, piracy, slavery,
theft, and extortion, as regular practices. In present
times, motives are presumably more self-controlled,
but external restraints upon them are none the less
daily in operation.

As will be seen, the economic system thrives on all
incentives, good or bad. In the case of those arising
from a wish to serve, little control is needed; sound
administration by itself is adequate to draw from them
all the productive power they can give. But where

acquisition is the chief aim, special arrangements are
needed in the system for preventing the direct expression of the motive, and for conducting it by indirect
channels into a constructive use. The system does,
in fact, possess arrangements for such control; otherwise it could not have come into being. Two main
elements in the scheme of control may be distinguished.

The first is the legal system. The law, built up
through generations, has succeeded with considerable
efficiency in blocking the most serious of the illicit
outlets for self-interest. It has constituted itself, so
to speak, the " container " of this motive. It has
checked leakages by way of theft and fraud and by
undue oppression. Thus, whenever any man now
desires to serve himself, the only way left open to
him is to apply himself to work, rendering services to
others, and in return receiving the service he personally desires : a devious method, but the only one
which the law leaves open.

The details of the law are woven round two main
bulwarks : the " right of property," and the " right
of free contract." The function of the " right of
property," under which all legally accumulated wealth
is protected from being vicariously raided, is to permit
the amassing of capital and to encourage saving.
The " right of free contract " ensures that when goods
are produced and amassed their exchange shall be
effected under freedom from either duress or fraud.
Without these two main features in the legal frame-

work of control, any economic system in which self-interest is the leading motive would rapidly disintegrate.

The second method whereby the economic system extracts service from the self-interested is more fortuitous. There has emerged, at a fairly early stage in the development of economic life, a condition customarily described as " division of labour "—a condition under which men individually specialise in the production of one single branch of goods or services, and offer their one product in exchange for the innumerable goods they themselves desire. In the present civilised community a man could barely subsist without accepting this " division of labour " and becoming a specialist. Certainly, one who was self-interested would not think of rejecting it as a method. But, as already seen, this condition, when coupled with the law, places the self-interested person in the position that if he wishes to serve himself he must first serve others. He must produce goods to exchange with and satisfy the wants of others. The " division of labour " thus yields a situation in which the greatest acquisitions are to be made only through the greatest contributions. The more self-interested a man may be, the more he is driven to studying and satisfying the needs of the community. By this convenient paradox, the economic system exploits self-interest to the full, turning it to the advantage of society as a whole.

Moreover, the " division of labour " establishes a condition under which a man may be induced to create wealth in much greater quantities than he can consume it. Being often in a position to command large forces of men and capital, a business manager may create many times the amount of wealth he could produce unaided. On the other hand, his personal consuming power reaches a fairly early limit. Thus, many who may have started their careers with hopes focussed mainly on their own advance, and have succeeded in erecting immense organs of production, have ended by being amongst society's first bene-factors—essentially because under the " division of labour " they have been able to produce much more than they could consume.

Whatever else may be said about the economic system, there can be no denying its extreme adapt-ability. By yet another paradox, it succeeds in placing power in the hands of those most intent on serving. It has been shown a few lines earlier that the greatest acquisitions can be made only through the greatest contributions. It is true, conversely, that whoever *begins* by being anxious to contribute, tends to be the very person to whom wealth flows. There can be no more profit-yielding asset in a firm than the goodwill arising from the belief that the firm's first aim is to give value. The belief breeds custom, the firm tends to grow, and it becomes its own advertise-ment. The initial will to contribute is then reinforced by the power to contribute; and the power increases.

Thus, by one process or another, the system tends to gain from all types of motive. The character of the motive seems to be of little account, in the material sense; provided it is cogent, the system will draw from it a full harvest. And the way it succeeds in this is, partly through the legal system, which controls any tendency for acquisition to find direct expression, and partly through the " division of labour " and the system of exchanging goods, which convert contributors into acquisitors, and acquisitors into contributors, and end by drawing contribution from all, whether their motive is towards gain or giving.

The " Behaviour " of the System.

For the rest, the system is perhaps best regarded as a series of business "habits." Those engaged in the system, being urged on by powerful incentives and disciplined by various legal rules, have developed certain universal modes of action, or business practices, the sum total of which constitutes the " behaviour " of the system.

These practices or habits, which are themselves far too great in number for separate description or even for enumeration, may for convenience be classified and in general described under three main headings : habits of conduct; habits in the use of economic mechanism; and, finally, habits of thought. Under these headings the attempt will be made to select and briefly explain the more outstanding of the remaining features of the system.

Habits of Conduct.

Amongst the most important of those business usages which have a special social bearing is that of " competition." The habit of competition, between employer and employer, or between worker and worker, appears to be derived as a part consequence of the division of labour. As soon as men become specialists in the production of one type of goods and exchange these goods in the market, persons with like talents or like produce find themselves competing with one another in the market. Division of labour inevitably implies a certain degree of competition, at least as between labourers and, where there is free enterprise, as between employers.

There will be occasion later for inquiring more closely into the actual nature of competition; at this stage little more is intended than to draw attention to and classify it. As far as may be judged from historical record, competition appears to have attained no great intensity until the Industrial Revolution; until then, markets were small, local monopoly was frequent, and mutual assistance within the monopoly most urgent. With the increasing size of industrial units and the widening of their markets, there has, however, been an initial tendency for producers to vie with each other in a more dynamic and acute struggle for the market. Similarly, the growth in the number of employed persons at first caused workers to be pitted against one another more keenly in their search for work. Twentieth-century developments have reversed this tendency, however, and competition has been replaced to a considerable extent by co-operation, owing to the growth of combinations amongst both employers and employed. In spite of this reversal, competition is still so general that it may justly be regarded as one of the outstanding features of the present system.

A further " habit of conduct " which calls for special mention here is that of " the employment of one group by another." This again is to some extent related to the division of labour, since it implies the rise of some specialists and the fall of others, and the absorption of the function of control by those who rise. But the chief significance of this habit, under which one group of persons agrees to take orders from, and in some ways subject itself to another, rests in its having led to the emergence of two distinct economic classes. It has produced a condition under which the community is divided against itself, since the two groups find themselves definitely in conflict on certain issues. In particular, conflict arises over the division of the joint product of the two groups;

and so long as the habit persists under which one
group employs the other, the problem of securing a
satisfactory division of the product must arise in
much the same form.

In other words, the employment of one group by
another has given birth to the wages system, with all
the difficulties which that implies in the matter of
finding a just relation between wages and profits,
and between one wage and another. It has created
a situation in which friction readily arises and in
which anything of the nature of permanent settlement is extremely difficult.

From these two outstanding " habits of conduct "
there have developed innumerable others. Competition has led to its own partial defeat, or modification, or regulation, through such further habits
as the setting up of employers' pools, cartels, trusts
and affiliations; the adoption of various forms of
partnership and company organisation; the regulation of patents and inventions; and the evolution of
trade customs, marketing traditions, sales methods,
and elaborate rules of business management. Similarly, the " employment of one group by another "
has been followed by the formation of craft and trade
unions and of employers' organisations; the elabora-
tion of different methods of wage-payment; the
establishment of arbitration, conciliation, and medi-
ation systems for the settlement of grievances; the
growth of apprenticeship schemes and the control of

labour movement; and the development of scientific management in all its forms.

All these are essentially habits. They are customary, accepted ways of conduct, and may be regarded as forming part of the superstructure or outward " behaviour " of the economic system.

Attention is to be confined here, however, almost exclusively to the two main habits, " competition " and " the employment of one group by another." The reason for this is partly that these seem to be central to others in the general texture of the system, and partly that they have far-reaching social implications.

Habits in the Use of Economic Mechanism.

There are certain instruments in use by industry which play an almost indispensable rôle in aiding the production and sale of goods. The regular use of any such instruments may be regarded as a habit, and as forming a part of the " behaviour " of the system, in the same way as any business habit described above.

The chief instrument of all is " money." Under this term is included not only coins, but also currency and bank notes, cheques and bills of exchange—every instrument, in fact, which civilised communities have devised for easing the interchange of goods.

Money is one of the earliest economic inventions of man, and may be regarded as perhaps the first mark of political civilisation, in that it implies some degree of faith in, and allegiance to the governing power which issues the currency. Its uses are so great that they are held to be indispensable. In the analogy between the economic system and a machine, money is sometimes regarded as the oil which lubricates the parts. But it is more than lubricant. It plays a rôle almost equal to, and corresponding with that of the transport system. Whenever goods are conveyed in one direction, money passes in the other. It is used as a means of moving the goods from producer to consumer, fully as much as is the physical means of transfer; and when money is reduced in supply at any stage, the immediate effect is almost exactly the same as if a portion of the country's rolling-stock had been destroyed.

A further feature of the money system is that it gives rise, in turn, to another element of economic mechanism—the price system. In any community in which money is in general use all articles for sale must be priced; and the fact of their being priced yields several specific advantages. Chief amongst these is that it enables consumers to make the best use of their incomes, distributing their purchases according to the cost of the articles. It also enables producers to determine which lines of production may most advantageously be developed.

The price system in turn gives rise to the profit system. When articles are sold at a given price, and the materials, labour and services required for their production are also priced, the difference between the sale price and the cost price yields profit.

It will be necessary later, when the problem of what is good and what is bad in the economic system is being examined, to go more fully into the relationships between the money, price and profit mechanisms, and to indicate their separate functions. The present task being rather that of classifying them, it is relevant only to note that, strictly speaking, the use of these three pieces of economic mechanism might be regarded as a " habit of conduct," and be included as such above. There seems some advantage to be gained, however, in discussing them apart, in that they are essentially instruments, and that, in consequence, any defects arising in connection with them must result less from their use than from their abuse.

Habits of Thought.

It is inevitable that any economic system will become surrounded by a philosophy peculiar to itself. For whenever an individual working in the system wishes to make a decision whether any line of conduct is right or wrong, his first test is the pragmatic one : How will it work ?   Will it pay ?   And since the test is applied in the conditions in which he is living at the time, it becomes, in reality : How will it work *in the existing economic order ?*

Thus, whatever the system may be, it supplies the basis for all judgments. It tends to mould and consolidate opinion along certain grooves and to establish " habits of thought " which, woven together, form the popular philosophy of the system.

*   *   *   *   *

The purpose of this bare outline of the present economic system, indicating that it comprises, first, a basic motive, secondly, a series of controls which regulate that motive, and, thirdly, certain characteristic habits or outward " behaviour," has been mainly to provide the framework into which more elaborations may be built later. But even on the basis of this short sketch, it may be permissible to throw out certain preliminary suggestions.

In the first place, since it is evident that not only is the system a thing of many parts, but also that these parts are in various ways related to each other and are mutually dependent, any proposed modification of the system must take full account of the reactions which the change of one part may have on others. And any new system which may be proposed must be tested not merely on the virtues of its several parts, but also on the manner in which they all " hang together." The economic system is organic. It performs its productive function through a vast number of interlocking processes. What is crucial, therefore, for the efficiency of any system, is that there shall be a true co-ordination between all processes.

A second thought is this : that, since the association

c

between the different parts of the system is so intimate, a reasonable anticipation may be formed that the correction of the system will rest, not in the abolition and reconstruction of the whole, but in the treatment of certain parts alone which at present are diseased and are spreading contagion to the rest.

CHAPTER II

THE FOUNDATIONS OF THE SYSTEM

IT is not intended here, nor would it seem possible, to attempt any account of the historical growth of the economic system, but only to show what are the main supports which strengthen and sustain the system as it is at present. The aim in view will be to reveal what are the chief factors which give the system its existing form, and will tend to perpetuate it in this form. Such a study of the " foundations " of the system is an indispensable first step in any discussion of its reconstruction. For it would be manifestly unreasonable to suggest any such reconstruction without learning first what are the defences which the present system may erect, and what is the nature of the supports which may have to be replaced.

The discussion will range mainly on the belief that the economic system is the direct issue from, and remains dependent on, human character.

The inability to discuss such a theme historically does imply, necessarily, a certain weakness of treatment. The appeal to history is required to show environment: that is, the nature of the conditions and setting in which the system has through time been formed or moulded. It is a commonplace of psychology that the conduct of an individual depends, first, on his inherited character; secondly, on his educational and physical environment—the conditions which through life have encircled him. It should similarly be a commonplace that the economic system, which is the conduct of individuals multiplied, must depend, first, on the character of the people, and secondly, on their wider environment. The only relevant difference between the way of action of the individual and that of the economic system as a whole, is that the system has continuous life. Because it has continuous life its present form may depend to some extent on things which occurred centuries ago— say, the Renaissance, or the laws of the Normans and Angevins. It is for this reason that an adequate explanation of the system's origins can be given only with the aid of history. For completeness it would be necessary to show how, down the ages, human character has reacted to environment, and has led to the formation of an economic system, and how this system has itself become part of the environment of the ensuing generations, influencing their character and being influenced in turn by new changes in their outlook due, say, to religious or political developments. The reactions have been unremitting between these two factors, character and environment, and their resultant is, through an inevitable process, the economic system.

Because the historical approach is denied us, the argument here will have to rest on one pillar alone. It will be necessary to assume human character as something given, and show that the system must result from, and conform to it. The various features of the system will again be passed in review, to illustrate that, had men's character and outlook differed materially from what they have so far been, every principal feature would have shown some difference in its development.

The Motive of Industry.

It is self-evident at the outset that the source from which the economic system draws its basic motive power is some element in character. Man works to satisfy some urge within him; and whatever urge stands out most prominently in the personal fibre of the majority must form the main support for industry in general.

The question of securing a change of motive depends therefore on the possibility of changing human nature. Many in present times seem ready to deny this possibility, and feel that the factors which make man's psychology are permanent and immutable. They would imply not only that the main forces which now govern action, whether of the business man or the employee or the professional worker, are founded mainly on the urges underlying self-interest, but also that there is little likelihood of changing these. These urges are part of the seed, and the seed, they say, is changeless.

There can be no question that the grip of self-interest (the precise meaning of which must be considered later) is exceedingly tenacious; for its foundations are laid in a series of ever-present and compelling bodily cravings. Moreover, what is in the body is not only an unrelenting urge affecting the conduct of the individual; it is present for all persons and for every generation, and compels recognition as a permanent social force. Self-interest of the most physical type has, therefore, a long future before it.

It does not necessarily follow, however, that because self-interest has a psychological basis which is permanent, it will always be dominant. Numerous forces may be assembled to reduce its strength and give other incentives the greater influence. Amongst such forces some are already known with definite assurance— education and religion, for instance—whilst others remain potential and more in the realm of speculation. It is impossible as yet to say to what conclusions the study of eugenics may lead, nor to forecast the ultimate value of experiments in suggestion and in the untapped realm of mind energy. But there is evidently a shrewd suspicion among scientists, amounting to a conviction with some, that, biologically, man is still

in his adolescence. They can point to numerous
untested powers waiting in his armoury.[1]

Turning to the least speculative realm, that of
education, we shall see that, so far, there have been
serious drags upon human evolution even through this
process. Up to the present the surplus powers of
nations, instead of being applied to development that
is constructive and educative, have to a large extent
been squandered in wars. Moreover, the energies
which remained have been not too well directed;
various plausible ideals, woven around semi-virtuous
sentiments such as empire, have held the thoughts of
educators, have given the directive to their teaching,
and have so monopolised the public mind as to prevent
its seeing what are the objectives intrinsically worth
attaining. Only when there is no more war and no
more fear of war will these ideals begin to fade and
others take their place. This stage cannot be so
many decades distant, it would seem, if for no other

---

[1] It would be relevant to quote from Jeans :

" In all probability the life in front of the human race must enormously
exceed the short life behind it. A million million years hence, so far as we
can foresee, the sun will probably still be much as now, and the earth will be
revolving round it much as now. The year will be a little longer, and the
climate quite a lot colder, while the rich accumulated stores of coal, oil, and
forest will long have been burnt up; but there is no reason why our descendants should not still people the earth. Perhaps it may be unable to support
as large a population as now, and perhaps fewer will desire to live on it. On
the other hand, mankind, being three million times as old as now, may—
if the conjecture does not distress our pessimists too much—be three million
times as wise.

" Looked at on the astronomical time-scale, humanity is at the very
beginning of its existence—a new-born babe, with all the unexplored
potentialities of babyhood."—(Eos, pp. 11, 12.)

reason than that progress in the science of slaying in the long run itself militates against war. War becomes unhealthy even for fools and criminals. Emancipation from the fear of war should mark a new point of departure in man's development. Nations which have previously spent excess energies in the attempt to crush each other will have these powers freed for other ends, and the only other end remaining will be the perfecting of society.

One immediate result should be the concentration of interest upon both popular and specialised education. Sooner or later a type of education should emerge which will raise the mind to its due position of ascendancy over those bodily enslavements which give self-interest its peculiar power. One may reasonably look forward to a system of instruction the keynote of which will be that of enhancing not merely the range and quality of the mind, but also its determination of character and its mastery over conduct.

Character, at least, is a thing dynamic. If different types of education and environment produce different types of character in the present, concentration on that educational method which yields the highest satisfaction now will lift the average character of the future. Better methods will raise it further.

If it were not so—and if the proposition which this chapter aims to demonstrate is true, namely, that the character of the people determines the nature of the economic system—then there could be no prospect of altering the system at any future time.

So far, however, only one point in the demonstration has been noted, and that self-evident : the basic *motive* of industry must be some chief constituent in human character.

The Legal Controls.

It has been seen earlier that, whatever may be the motive actuating those engaged in industry, whether it be egotistic or altruistic, this motive would probably operate in a promiscuous or disorderly way unless subject to some regulation; and that, for this reason, the legal system has been set up in support of the existing order, and a code of rules established for determining the limits within which man's present motive may find expression.

Since the code of rules has for its specific purpose the regulation of the motive, the nature of the code itself must depend primarily on the nature of the motive to be controlled. Thus, if the main principles established in the present legal system are the " right of property " and the " right of free contract," it is because these are the particular principles required to place the rein on the motive of self-interest. And so long as self-interest remains dominant, something akin to these two rights must inevitably be maintained.

This belief may be illustrated by reference to a situation which has arisen and may arise readily in a new-established colony. In a group of early settlers, banded for mutual aid against danger and a rigorous climate, such a spirit of solidarity may grow that the colony forms spontaneously into a communism. Each member, returning from the forest or water's edge, throws into the common pool his gain and takes from it what is needed to keep him efficient, having regard to the fact that others depend on the same supply. He contributes all he can so that the reserve stocks or capital of the group may grow. In such conditions, with all members of the group perforce altruists and anxious to build up the position of the whole settlement, there can be no purpose in a "right of property." Property is universally respected, and the colony can work with no legal restraint of any kind. But immediately the character of the settlers were to decline, the situation would change as regards property.

If only one member of the group became idle and predatory, something would have to be done to prevent his becoming parasitic upon the rest. Some defence of the common fund would be necessary and at least a right of *communal* property established. Then, were the character or outlook of the colonists to change still further, so that, on the one hand, a considerable number of them became lax in their efforts to produce and, on the other, the more vigorous wished to cast off their responsibility for others, the whole position would change. The emergence of self-interest in this way would lead to the establishment by the stronger group of a right of *private* property under which they would guarantee protection to each man of whatever he was able to produce himself or gain by fair exchange.

The situation is substantially the same in present times. The " right of property " as now established owes its origin essentially to the self-interest of the majority who are desirous of protecting their produce against the self-interested attacks of the minority. It is the self-interest of the minority which makes *some* defence of property necessary, and it is the self-interest of the majority which makes this defence take the form of a right of *private* property.

It may thus be said that the right of property, and, indeed, all legal regulations, have their ultimate basis in human character. This might be still further illustrated by showing how, especially in the past century, changes in the general social outlook of civilised communities have been accompanied by corresponding changes in the right of property. Intense individualism has given place to a gradually increasing social consciousness, an appreciation by the stronger of their responsibility for the less fortunate; and this has resulted in progressive changes in the right to do what one will with one's own, with factories, with land, with exceptional profits and income, and with inheritance. Taxation laws, factory laws, land regulations, minimum-wage legislation, and the setting up of innumerable inspectorates in the last fifty years have involved wide changes in the privileges and rights of those who hold possessions. Further substantial modifications of the " right of property " may be expected in the future, together with changes in the more detailed legal framework of the system. But whatever form the " right of property " and the " right of free contract " may take, this will depend in the future, as it has done in the past, on the development of the general outlook and character of the people.

Business Habits.

There remains for consideration the outward " behaviour " of the system. This has been divided here into various categories of " habits," the term " habits " being used specifically because it throws out at once the idea of action based on character.

Competition, the first feature singled out under this classification, is clearly a habit based on character. It is a regular mode of conduct followed in business, and whilst arising, as has been seen, from the division of labour, it owes its peculiar intensity to psychic forces. The spirit of competition is so powerful and deep-seated, in fact, that one might be tempted to regard it as instinctive; and although there would perhaps seem more justification for considering it merely as one form of expression of self-interest—the inflating of self *relatively* to others—the belief remains that its roots are firmly bedded in current human nature.

As regards the habit, " employment of one group by another," this, again, may have arisen, in the mechanical sense, from the division of labour, but it must also be attributed to distinct differences in the capacity of man to realise the future. Although in any community the members may begin with equal handicaps and work independently, certain of them with a strong consciousness of the future will make due provision for it by laying in food and implements; whilst others, with a feeling only of the present, will lead a hand-to-mouth existence. Then, when bad times come, the inevitable happens : those who do not have reserves seek out those who have and offer in exchange for food all that is left to them : their labour. Thus, the employment of one group by another may be, in its earliest inception, the result of differences in the capacity to sense the future. It may be but the parable of the wise and foolish virgins, writ large. Once formed, however, the habit tends to strengthen, and as industry becomes more complex the difficulty of changing from the employed to the employing class increases. The factor which now frequently determines the group into which a man will fall is merely the chance of birth : whether he is born with or without a heritage.

Habits in the Use of Economic Mechanism.

Many different aspects of human character have been reflected in the formation of the various mechanisms, or instruments, invented for giving greater ease or smoothness to production and trade. Particularly is this true of the money, price and profit mechanisms, described earlier. Each of these has involved the setting up of complex organisms as intrinsic parts of the industrial system. In the case of money, its service has been made efficient only through the establishment of the Mint and Treasury, the Banking system, the Stock Exchange and Foreign Exchange and all that is implied by the "City." The price and profit mechanisms have involved, in addition, an extensive system of audit and accountancy. Although these interwoven parts of the economic system may have arisen in some instances from the acquisitiveness of money-lenders, they could not have been established but for great ingenuity; nor could they have reached their present pitch without high standards of business faith and reliability. Man may be acquisitive; but in playing the acquisitive game he certainly plays to the rules.

Were the attempt made to penetrate still further into the habits and institutions which form the economic system, it would become increasingly apparent that their development has been due to many widely differing human traits. The responsibility has not always rested on self-interest, but frequently on courage, perseverance, foresight, and great genius. What is significant, however, is that it has always been some element in character. It is true that, as noted at the beginning, the system has emerged from character working in a particular environment, and that a different environment would have meant in some respects a different system. Mass-production methods, for instance, could never have replaced the handicraft system but for revolutionary discoveries of power and of resources. But given the contents of the earth and the fortunes of discovery and chance invention, the economic system has developed and assumed its present form essentially because men are as they are.

A Human Institution.

In brief, a conclusion is reached which, once seen, becomes a platitude : the economic system is human in every part. It is simply human character finding expression. Our excuse, if we have unduly laboured this point, is that, frankly, it is not seen. It may be abstractly accepted, but its significance is not gripped. The majority of us, when speaking of the " system," regard this as something imposed on the community from outside; an entity or organism having a life apart from the individuals that compose it. Thus we pour execration on the system, frequently oblivious

that the thing accused is nothing but the habits
in which we and fellow-sinners are indulging. Were
the system viewed more generally in this light,
our socialism might suffer less the paralysis of
inconsistency.

Again, the truism that the system is only human
habit is not seen, in that its corollaries are not seen.
This is especially so in the matter of projected altera-
tions to the system. There is no adequate recognition, for instance, that, just as the habits of a single
individual cannot be changed without the individual's
being himself converted to the change, so there can
be no transformation of the habits of all members of
the community unless an immediate and universal
reform is possible in the outlook of those members.
Proposals for altering the conduct of industry are
often made, and sometimes actually applied, in
complete disregard for the existence of a problem of
psychology and education. The question is not
asked : Can human nature rise to it ?

Even in proposed minor changes, such as the
nationalisation of an industry, the significance of the
human element is not safely to be ignored. In any
such case it would be necessary to decide whether, on
the one hand, a public board of directors, with assured
salaries and no personal stake in the fortunes of the
industry, could be relied upon to take risks judiciously,
to engage in active campaigns for the widening of
their markets and to do that which is especially dis-

tasteful—hold their subordinates, also with assured
salaries and little risk, to a vigorous prosecution of
the work. On the other hand, it would be necessary
to consider whether the large majority of employees,
in turn, would be public-spirited enough not to slacken
their pace when they realised that the new hierarchy was
perhaps less exacting and less disciplinarian than the old.

The inference here is not that human nature could
not, in fact, stand it, but merely that the question
must not be ignored. Neither is there any assertion
here that no change whatever can be made unless
preceded by a change in character. Changes in the
system may often be made in anticipation of, and
actually to facilitate, the requisite change in outlook.
For instance, a portion of the British coal mines
might be nationalised not merely in the expectation
that a sufficient number of socially-minded persons
might be found to direct the work and operate the
mines, but also to open special *opportunities* for such
persons to give full expression to their latent other-
interestedness. Only in this way can new " habits "
be established in place of the old.

One conclusion, however, which is of transcendent
importance for any practical programme of reform is
this : No change in the structure of the economic
system should be attempted which goes *radically*
beyond the powers of human character. Unspeakable
sufferings have resulted from the failure to realise
this principle at first in Russia. It is perhaps not

D

just to criticise the efforts of that country on the existing basis of knowledge, for contemporaneous information is invariably incomplete, if not perverted; neither is it just to criticise the executives who have had the daring to attempt the most far-reaching social reconstruction of the century. But, regarded impersonally as an experiment, the Russian revolution gave at the outset an appalling and, one hopes, a final proof of the need for realising human limitations in any projected economic change. Communism, which was the régime at first attempted, is essentially a spiritual ideal, and could only be made effective through universal altruism. To attempt to force it on a people at the point of the sword, as was done initially, is the most cynical form of contradiction. ″

It may be, perhaps, that it was necessary to overshoot to some extent the limit of what was ultimately possible, in order to be sure of making the maximum advance. And it is to be hoped therefore that in the process of reaction, which must follow any grant of individual freedom, the country will not be swung too far towards the opposite extreme, and that a position of stability may finally emerge in which Russian institutions will represent in some respects an advance on those of other countries. This result will depend essentially on how much the community as a whole has learnt from the turmoil and readjustments through which it has passed. If, in consequence of the mental upheaval which accompanies any widespread social change, and of the stupendous educational effort now being made, a new philosophy and a new outlook have developed affecting the masses of the people, then they may be capable of operating a system organically different from that of the rest of the Western world. If, on the other hand, no such development in outlook should take place, once the country overthrows the virtual dictatorship of an administration and returns to government by consent, the economic system will revert to substantially its initial form.

This is not a prophecy, but merely the statement of a law. When the economic system is seen exactly as it is—a complex of universal human " habits," every one of which has come into existence under the pressure of human motives, has been shaped by human minds, and has been adapted to meet both the strength and weaknesses of human character—the conclusion directly follows that to change the economic system *is* to change human character, and *vice versa*.

The practical conclusion to which such a concept leads is this. In order to produce any marked effect upon the economic system, the line of approach must be : first, to work out in detail the nature of the new system desired; secondly, to decide what qualities in human personality would be needed to ensure the effective operation of the system; and thirdly, to institute a widespread campaign of education to produce these qualities.

CHAPTER III

STRENGTH AND DEFECTS

THE third, and perhaps the most difficult stage in the analysis of the economic system is the examination of its various parts from the point of view of their inherent strength or weakness. The peculiar difficulty of this task rests in the fact that, in economic matters, there is found no authority as to what is good and bad. There can, for instance, be no privilege to say whether competition is good in itself, or profit, or the wages system. In all cases the appeal is to opinion; and opinions must differ according to the point of departure of each individual judge. Probably the most that may be expected towards agreement, therefore, is the general approval of some criterion—a criterion which would seem reasonable for testing the satisfactoriness of different features of the system—and the attempt to apply this in such a manner as to draw wide acceptance.

The criterion proposed, then, is: harmony. In other words, only those features of the system will be regarded here as sound and useful which tend towards its harmonious working.

Such a criterion is perhaps almost self-commending.

Any feature which lends harmony to the system must possess intrinsically the power to satisfy the majority working within the system. Further, a factor which increases harmony must thereby reinforce all tendencies towards co-operation and raise the efficiency of the system, so that, whatever may be the aims to be attained through it, they will be secured most effectively.

Given this as the central test, the task in what ensues will be to marshal for inspection once more the system's chief features, and decide in respect of each whether it yields harmony or disharmony. Subsidiary tests will be used at some points, but they will not perhaps be such as to raise controversy in their actual context.

THE MOTIVE OF INDUSTRY

Up to this stage the common view has been assumed here that the " average " motive of industry is self-interest; and little attempt has been made to determine either how far this is a sound view, or what precise meaning is implied by the term " self-interest." If, however, this motive is to be examined to discover within what limits it may, in itself, satisfy, the first step must be to define it. Self-interest may be expressed in various ways, some of its outlets being felt to be good and others bad. For instance, a person may work keenly, partly because he covets luxury, partly because he fears insecurity, partly because he is concerned for his dependents, and partly because he desires esteem. The questions arise : Which of these and other motives may be regarded as self-interest ? And how many of such expressions of self-interest are desirable ?

Perhaps these questions may be answered best if the attempt is made to penetrate to the roots of self-interest and discover something of its psychological basis. A motive can only be made clear in concept when described in relation to its origin. Hence the sound approach here will be to indicate, at the outset, the way in which self-interest is founded in the mind and in the body.

There is one form it takes, at once the most powerful and the least avoidable, which may be termed for convenience " natural " self-interest. This is the self-interest which is imposed upon a person by the claims of his body. (Throughout the term " natural " will be used here as being synonymous with " bodily." The body is a thing of nature, and its contents are in kind immutable. The mind, on the other hand, though in some ways tied to nature, has contents which are not immutable : ideas, for instance, which may be varied at the will of the educator. The compelling forces of the body are thus " natural "; those of the mind may be developed or " acquired.")

Of the bodily influences which cause men to be self-interested the most potent is the hunger drive. There can be no challenging the ultimate strength of hunger

as a force compelling men to work, since death is the
only alternative to its satisfaction. But, as a motive,
it operates considerably before actual want of food is
felt. The mere contemplation of the possibility of
hunger, or even of insufficiency, is much more powerful
as a means of driving men to work than all other
motives. Once this possibility is removed, however,
other factors rise in importance. Next in strength, all
psychologists agree, is the sex impulse. The sex
impulse arises, as does the hunger drive, from a
definite physiological state, the impelling force of
which may be judged, if from no other circumstance,
from its having throughout time been relied upon
alone for the continuance of human life. Then, on a
different plane, and much less imperious in their
ultimate command over conduct, are the demands of
the senses. There is at all times a certain appetite
for the pleasures of taste, hearing, sight and touch;
and if for a period these senses go unsatisfied there
arises a feeling somewhat akin to starvation. This
whole group of bodily impulses, hunger, sex, and the
lesser cravings of the senses, forms the powerful
combination of forces which lies at the basis of
" natural " self-interest.

Up to a point it is clearly inevitable to be self-
interested in this way, since the senses themselves
have a specific purpose and their satisfaction in some
degree is necessary for the individual's welfare or for
that of the race. But the place and purpose of this

motive are to be considered later; at this point the
desire is only to call attention to one of its origins, and
show its connection with industry. If an operative
works sedulously because he needs to afford more
food and drink or restrain less his physical life, this is
" natural " self-interest. Or if others are prompted by
thoughts of more spacious luxury, or comfortable
travel, or in general greater freedom in satisfying
sense urges, this also is " natural " self-interest.
Every motive may, in fact, be comprised under this
head if it comes from the desire to appease or gratify
or in any way give rein to a bodily impulse.

This type of self-interest is to be distinguished from
another form, " acquired " self-interest, which is a
mental rather than a physical development. Initially,
perhaps, arising from natural or bodily causes, this
second aspect of self-interest may be strengthened
through educational influences, and may be to that
extent " acquired." Some explanation is perhaps
needed. In earliest life a child forms in his mind a
" consciousness of self." Happenings around him
are all recorded on his senses, and are stored up in the
newly developing mind. He discovers wants within
him, and feelings about things he likes and dislikes.
These wants and feelings are registered directly in
himself, and not in others; and he thus begins to distinguish himself from other people. By virtue of
these separate, independent feelings, a " consciousness
of self " arises, something definitely mental. Some-

times this consciousness is so strong that it excludes from his mind the recognition of the existence of other people. That is, there is no true realisation that others have feelings or that they count at all.

" Consciousness of self " is thus a quality which all have inevitably at an early stage. The point of concern socially, however, is whether it develops into a balanced, moderate self-appreciation or whether it is magnified into obsession. And this depends on education. If the training at home or at school is such as to throw emphasis on a child's own wants, his own occupations, his own success and, ultimately, his own pre-eminence, it is inevitable that this initial natural tendency to be interested mainly in himself will be fostered and will grow into intense self-concentration. In all circumstances an individual thus mentally formed will think first of his own concerns, regarding himself and his rise to position as ends in themselves and pursuing these with a peculiar fanaticism.

Carried forward into industry, such an " acquired " self-interest may become a powerful incentive. It is this kind of motive which is operating, for instance, whenever a man works to improve his status. If he looks upon his trade as primarily a means for maintaining rank socially, or of levering himself into a new stratum, it is clearly this " acquired " sense of self as an end which is the driving power. Similarly, when a person is prompted to work by the hope of reaching a post of notoriety, or a certain prestige, this indicates that the same motive, the feeling of self as an end, is at work.

Sometimes " acquired " self-interest underlies the fear of losing employment. We are induced to strive because inefficiency may mean dismissal, and then, the raised eyebrows of friends. It is the faint scorn of neighbours that is the real dread of the unemployed.

Interest in self may readily expand into interest in the group surrounding self. Frequently the group is formed specifically to protect the interests of the individuals comprising it, as in the case, for instance, of the trade association or the state. In these instances, loyalty to the group may be expected to be at least as strong as loyalty to the self, and often it is much stronger.

" Group " self-interest, by reason of the good results it produces amongst those within the group, is usually regarded as itself virtuous. If *esprit de corps* and vigorous co-operation arise, these things in themselves are gains of the highest order. But the true measure of the virtue of " group " self-interest can only be made when the purposes of the group as a whole have been considered, together with its relationship to others outside. If its aim is merely to pool the interests of the members, the " group " self-interest which emerges is no more virtuous than the self-interest of each individual member. And if there is a

certain fantasy in imagining that one single individual is more important than all others, it is still
more fantastic, and immeasurably more dangerous,
to imagine that one group of individuals is more
important than all others. " Group " self-interest, to
take one example only, lies at the basis of all wars.

Such thoughts would seem to apply much less, if at
all, to the family. This case is one in which the group
surrounding self often comes to be regarded as
virtually *belonging to* the individual. It is not infre-
quent, for instance, for the family to appear in the
mind of the parent as his own product and property.
Thus the principle applies : " What is mine is part
of me." The parent will fight and work and deny
himself for his family because he feels his family to be
" of him." His son's failure is his own. His family's
want is his own lack and his own disgrace.

In the purely industrial sphere, the only form in
which " group " self-interest finds strong expression as
a motive seems to be that of interest for the family.
Most men are drawn to much increased effort when they
undertake to support others; and it is a familiar
experience that the moment at which a person settles
to work solidly coincides as a rule with the moment
when he accepts this added duty. Interest for the
group acts as a much more cogent spur than any
previously known care.

When the combined effect is considered of these
chief forms of self-interest—" natural " self-interest,

causing a person to seek physical ease and comfort; " acquired " self-interest, a form of self-concern which creates eagerness for position or social power; and " group " self-interest, impelling a man to spend himself for the home and children—it will be recognised that they represent a large part of the incentives at present driving industry. They are a powerful group. And if in the past industry has been a thing of prodigious strength and life, this is in no small measure due to the force of these incentives based on need and self.

It is due at least in part, however, to one more motive : that of the urge to add. Few seem to know with sureness from what this springs, least of all those who possess it. It is strangely present; and its power is fierce.

The Tests applicable to Motive.

These first thoughts on the meaning of different types of motive will make it possible to follow up now the main task of the chapter : that of examining the soundness of the various elements of the system. Concerning the first of these, the motive, it is suggested that self-interest is probably still the most widespread force in industry, and accordingly it is this which will receive chief attention in what follows.

In any attempt to judge a motive, it would seem necessary to make a distinction between the motive itself and the nature of its results. Frequently a motive may be entirely unexceptionable in its beginnings, and yet, if carried to extremes, may yield *some* adverse results.

In the case of self-interest, quite evidently the motive cannot be bad in itself. In essence, " natural " self-interest implies simply the desire to satisfy those urges which were set there to be satisfied. It means the will to appease wants, the appeasing of which serves some fundamental purpose in creation and procreation. Thus, it must inevitably be " good " to satisfy the hunger drive, since otherwise all life would cease. The same may be said, and more, in the case of the sex impulses; for by strange magic these are not only the basis of new life, but also of the power to see beauty. Art, and most creativeness, and much of the emotional warmth of life seem to depend directly upon the same source as that from which the race springs. Thus if by " natural " self-interest is meant, in this sphere, the will both to express and replenish life, it must be a two-fold good.

Much the same thought would seem true of the urge to satisfy other senses. Whoever strives for the fruits of sight, touch, or hearing is showing simply an eagerness to enjoy. He shows a will to live and be refreshed. All life, indeed, revolves on the things grasped by the senses; and to crave more of these is, essentially, a welcoming, a gratefulness. In itself, this " natural " self-interest must be good, since it is the basis of the appreciation of all experience and of the power to exchange and multiply experience.

It seems perhaps less easy to show enthusiasm in the case of "acquired" self-interest, but even this is obviously desirable in its beginning. No person would be able to become interested in humanity without first being interested in himself as one representative of it, and the only representative whose being he may hope to understand completely. He is the only individual of whom he can make an intimate study; and until, from self-study, he develops understanding, he can be of little help, humanly, to others.

"Group" self-interest, most often, arises from a parental instinct which, again, exists for an intended service, and leads to expressions having their own deep inwardness.

It would be unthinking, therefore, to regard self-interest as, in itself, not good. All that may be held against the motive is that, when carried to extremes, it may bring results which hurt. Whereas under restraint it yields results which are only good, other results of an adverse kind may arise when it is allowed free rein. It is only the excess of self-interest which injures. Thus, the ideal in any society would be to allow this motive expression up to the point at which it yields its maximum good. At some point it would require to be checked, being "disciplined" by some other motive, if the best result is to be reached.

It may be emphasised at this point, then, that if, in the remainder of these pages, reference is made to self-interest as a cause of harm, the meaning implied invariably is " inadequately restrained " self-interest. Indeed, it is by reason of the belief that this motive at present far over-reaches the point at which all is good, and in some way maims the economic system, that it is held in question. In the first place, when it is carried thus to extremes, it fails utterly to satisfy the chief criterion adopted at the outset here : the criterion of " harmony." The motive is, in excess, the one destroyer of harmony. To be self-interested without restraint is to wish to surround oneself with acquisitions—wealth and power—and if all men draw from the same supply of these, their aims unavoidably conflict. The greater satisfaction of the one means the less satisfaction of the other; and discord must follow. Similarly, to be self-interested is to wish for unrestricted movement, or full licence for self-expression; but when one group arrogates to itself more liberty, it tramples on the liberty of others. Men live in crowds; if some use their elbows, other suffer.

Self-interest, unrestrained, is directly responsible—and, on consideration, solely responsible—for all forms of social unrest. In civil life it is prevented from creating excessive friction by the intervention of law, which sets up barriers between the self-interests of different people, and has the means of holding the barriers in position. In industry, however, it is difficult for the law to intervene everywhere. Up to the present it has proved impossible to decide extensively by law how industries should divide their earnings amongst the parties; and many other features of industrial agreements have shown themselves to be as yet beyond legal definition. In consequence, these issues continue to be settled by the primitive method of trial of strength, on the principle that "might is right," a principle which must bring disharmony.

The chief test by which the motive of self-interest is to be judged, however, is its effect upon the rest of the economic system. As observed earlier, the motive permeates every separate activity in the system; it operates through, and has largely been responsiblé for, each of the various "habits" which have emerged; and according to its effect on and through these habits it must mainly be judged.

Thus any conclusion to be reached must await the discussion of the various other features of the system. There are two points, however, to be urged provisionally at this stage. First, no complaint can be laid against self-interest in its beginnings, since it is a thing of Nature leading to expression, art, and a wide appreciation. Secondly, when carried to excess, it defeats much of its original beauty; it leads to a form of gluttony, and to brawling among the gluttons. By its very nature, it must in excess cause discord.

The Legal Controls

In the earlier discussion of the origins of the economic system, it was seen that the setting up of the " right of property " and other similar legal principles is a direct corollary of the existence of an excess of self-interest. So long as there remain in the community any individuals whatever with predatory tendencies, some legal barriers must be set up to hold them in check and prevent their destroying property. This is necessary in the interests not only of the community, but also of the individuals themselves, who otherwise would develop into social parasites. The legal system is, in fact, a bar to the general outbreak of antisocial habits.

Such an argument, however, justifies only the establishment of a " right of *communal* property "; it shows the need for protecting property in general, but not necessarily for permitting its accumulation in private hands. Thus, whereas the " right of *communal* property " may be dismissed at once as raising no problem whatever as regards its acceptance, the " right of *private* property " presents a special aspect and raises various controversial issues. The discussion here will accordingly be confined to the questions centring on the maintenance of property in the hands of single individuals.

E

The Right of Private Property.

The complete abolition of private property of all kinds is, it seems, almost unthinkable. Such items as clothes, certain instruments of art or sport, books, photographs, trophies and all possessions which form, as it were, part of the very personality of the individual, can never be made communal in any sense. The restriction which can be put upon the ownership of private property must necessarily be incomplete; and the problem resolves itself, therefore, into determining what is the precise extent of restriction, if any, which it would be desirable to apply. In order to provide a basis for such a decision, some consideration must first be given to the abuses arising out of the *unrestricted* ownership of private property.

These abuses, it may be said, are in many cases indirect and are so varied that it will be impossible here to do more than point to the more serious of them. The task will be, not so much to describe the ill-effects themselves, which are common experience, as to note the manner in which they are directly or indirectly related to the right of private property. Four main abuses of this right may be enumerated :—

1. A first direct effect of the power to amass property without limit is that it encourages competitive display, together with the setting up of class distinctions. The possession of wealth creates for many an irresistible temptation to parade it; in fact, for some there is

little other purpose in gaining wealth than to spread
it before others. The right of private property opens
the way, then, to a peculiarly sordid form of rivalry—
a rivalry in which each displays his material worth,
thinking it the emblem of real distinction. This form
of competition, ignoble though it may be, would
perhaps be of little seriousness were it not that the
competitors are graded and allotted to a caste according to their wealth. Class distinctions have emerged
in the present social system, founded largely on
possession; thus, aristocracy becomes inseparable
from plutocracy, and the so-called upper, middle, and
lower classes are distinguished almost exclusively by
their means.

The formation of social class distinctions of any
kind would seem to be the very negation of the idea of
society, in that it not only divides the community into
different camps, but actually segregates certain of
them as being unfit for association with the rest. Such
an implied slur can only create resentment among
those disdained. To them the presumption of
superiority and inferiority is alone an offence; but
there is an added sting, making the situation scarcely
tolerable, when the presumed difference in social
fitness is based on inequalities of income—a condition
which itself is regarded as gross injustice.

2. Whatever may be the grievances arising out of the
existence of private property, they tend to become
more firmly established with time. Property has a

considerable power of self-maintenance and self-accumulation; for the ownership of property is itself the handle opening the door to greater ownership. Some ownership of capital is necessary at the outset to permit a man to enter business and thus set on foot the process of making profit. Later, when his capital holdings become much larger, savings out of surplus income become almost automatic, and wealth increases without effort, and by steady progression. It is due to this self-accumulative power of property that the immense disparities in income which now exist have arisen. And it is due to this, therefore, that full rein is given to many of the most serious offences of the system. In particular, it is the self-accumulative power of property which leads to the existence side by side of slums and mansions, and makes more acute the sense of poverty by throwing it into contrast with extravagance.

3. One direct corollary of the unrestricted right of private property is the right of inheritance; and from this follow various further grievances. Any leader of enterprise who has amassed wealth through his own resourcefulness and effort may become the object of respect. But this is not so in the case of his heirs. There is a bias against them at the outset because they have attained position through no merit of their own; and this bias grows when, as not infrequently happens, they show themselves below the calibre of the parent and unqualified to carry his responsibility. Often,

however, it is a case not so much of being unqualified, as of being unconcerned; after living in greater luxury and having acquired a taste for social amenities, they have only a lukewarm interest left for business.

From the purely economic point of view the inheritance of industry by those not interested in industry is probably the most serious weakness in the present system. And although the generalisation made here, if it were not a generalisation, would be unfair to many brilliant exceptions, it does not seem unreasonable to suppose that the longer the hereditary principle persists the more handicapping will it be in its general effect on industry. In a newly expanding country its influence is perhaps hardly perceptible; but where the possibility of expansion is limited, as it is in the older European countries, the selection of leadership becomes determined more and more on the hereditary principle, and thus adds to the existing tendency to stagnation.

4. There is, finally, a more indirect way in which the right of private property is injurious. It sets a false standard of generosity. If it is regarded as a " right," an element of justice, that all should retain whatever goods they lawfully acquire, then the sacrifice of even a small fraction of these goods, voluntarily, is ranked as " generosity." For most of us the process of becoming generous is somewhat devious. We begin by raising our own station and level of comfort until personal ambition is satisfied. Then we make pro-

vision for the coming years and for the succeeding generation. Then, the nest having been well feathered both for the present and for the future, we become " generous." Out of our excess we make munificent offerings to the poor. And no matter how big the surplus, the rendering up of the smallest item of it is looked upon as " generosity."

One chief cause of this distortion of ideas is the right of private property. By establishing that all ours is ours by right, it raises our puny self-denial to the level of high merit, and blinds us to the appreciation of real need.

The spirit of generosity and, in general, the attitude of society with regard to the obligations of the strong and wealthy group to those less favoured, has a deep economic significance. It is the one determinant of the extent to which income can be *re*distributed through taxation. When the average level of generosity is low, not only is it difficult to secure the passage through Parliament of new fiscal measures, but also when higher taxes are in fact imposed the effort of evasion increases. Moreover, if the wealthy are not prepared to make any personal sacrifice, taxes tend to be paid rather out of savings than through the reduction of personal expenditure, and the decline in savings, in turn, hampers the development of industry. . . . In another, entirely different sphere of income distribution, that of copartnership and profit-sharing, the success or failure of any scheme for the division of profits depends primarily on whether it can be regarded as truly magnanimous. It is on the growth of the spirit of generosity that ultimately depends the extent to which profit-sharing can become a prominent feature of industrial organisation.

Thus, whilst the amassing of wealth under the protection of the right of private property leads in the first place to prodigious differences in ownership and income, the possibility of securing a redistribution through taxation or through profit- and ownership-sharing schemes is limited by our meagre standards of generosity; the meagreness of these standards being due, again, to the general belief that to retain property is a " right."

The Uses of Private Ownership.

From even a brief summary such as this it is clear that the right of private property opens the way to many of the worst results of the economic system : the vanities of display; the emergence of class distinctions; gross inequalities in wealth and income; the selection of industrial leadership on the basis of inheritance; and the setting of false standards of social obligation. It is not surprising that communists and other extreme idealists should make the right of property their foremost point of attack.

Nevertheless, these abuses cannot be said to arise *inevitably* out of the right of private property. It is only because the property is in the hands of a community of people who are for the most part stupid and arrogant that it gives these results. The " right " itself is permissive only. It makes the abuses legally possible; it gives full rein to them; it even sets the stamp of convention on certain of them. But it does not *produce* them. The right of private property is not the fundamental cause.

Display, for instance, is not caused by, but only permitted by the right of ownership. The " cause " is human vanity. The same may be said of class distinctions. There is no reason why any person, merely because he has wealth, should either flaunt it publicly or regard himself as *ipso facto* in a class apart from those with less. There is no reason why he should not, on the contrary, devote the whole of his possessions to the furtherance of some external or social aim, and class himself merely as one of the undiscriminating tribe of Abou Ben Adhem.

Nor does the right of private property necessarily compel the belief that " generosity " consists in any partial surrender of this right. The whole of the Western world, with its established philosophy of possession, may be ready to acclaim as generous a man's sacrificing his comfortable surplus; but there is no reason why the man himself, or any other, should not have a larger view.

Logically, a " right " cannot in any circumstances be a " cause." At the most it is an open gate—an inlet to a certain field of opportunity. And, in order to prevent the abuse of the opportunity, there are two possible ways of action. One is to close the gate : abolish the right. The other is to cure the *motive* of those who pass through, the real " cause " of the trouble, and thus ensure that they use their opportunity to good purpose. The second method is the ideal if the opportunity is essentially worth preserving. As will be seen, the opportunities afforded by the use of private property seem well worth being preserved.

It is clear, as already noted, that personal belongings are up to a point quite indispensable in any civilised group. Clothes and trophies and all things pertaining to the person or to the home, or sports, or hobbies must remain very largely private property. Then, in addition to these bare necessaries, there is a wide range of property, such as houses, private gardens, vehicles, or books, from which greater value may often be gained if they are privately rather than communally owned, in that when they are the recognised property of the individual they may be made to reflect his special taste and feeling, and become, in fact, an enhancement of his personality. They may be part of the means whereby he develops self-expression, and thus interprets himself to the outer world.

The unique virtue of property is its power to symbolise. For those who wish to maintain themselves in contact with some historic event, or current movement, or some special interest, there is often a need for personal collections to make the contact vivid : thus a souvenir in private hands may be of untold value. Then, through its power to symbolise, personal property may add a certain depth of quality to exchanges. A well-chosen gift may be the only possible embassy of an inner thought; even the destruction of something owned, a cask of ointment, may have a meaning for which there is no other method of expression. Were private property to be completely disavowed, there would be removed a power of self-interpretation without which human intimacy would be much the poorer.

The only way in which private property can be judged in true perspective would seem to be through attempting to visualise its rôle in the ideal state. As far as any imperfect state is concerned, private property is in any case inevitable; that is, it will unavoidably emerge wherever (given a condition of government by consent) the predominant motive is extreme self-interest. Since this motive implies as its central expression the striving for acquisition of private property, the first thing which the members of the community will do, if they are self-governing, will be to ensure the protection of private property. They will not only set up a protective right to render their property safe, but they will continue to use and abuse it in much the same way as has been indicated above. The ultimate test of the inherent right or wrong of private property must therefore be applied, not in the conditions of an imperfect state where it will almost

certainly exist and be abused, but in the assumed conditions of the ideal state, in which the motive of " contribution " would predominate amongst the members
—their primary aim being to further purposes which
were common to society as a whole.

In a State so composed, private ownership would
presumably be without serious drawbacks, since things
transcending possession would determine the use and
the usefulness of property. Members would regard
themselves as trustees of their property, limiting their
personal use of it, and applying the surplus to the
common need or interest. The one outstanding problem which would then arise would be : Up to what
point can the common aims of a society be achieved
more effectively through the administering of surplus
earnings by the individuals themselves who make the
earnings, than through their being pooled in a central
fund ?

This is a problem which will have to be considered
later, but it may be said at the outset that *some*
independent control of surplus earnings by those who
make the earnings is desirable. The only person who
really respects any piece of property as it should be
respected is he who has the travail of producing it.
Those who spend other people's earnings, no matter
how excellent their motives, have not the sense of the
effort involved in producing them, and tend to become
extravagant. The further the distance of the administration which spends from the controlling influence of

the individuals who earn, the greater is the probability of loss of economy in expenditure.

Thus, in the ideal economic state private property would in all probability still subsist; the chief change would be that it would not be abused. Private property would be regarded as a more effective means of attaining certain ends than communal property; and on this ground alone it would be retained.

The right of inheritance would, it seems, almost certainly be abolished. The selection of those who were to be entrusted with the administration of capital could hardly be left to the chances of birth in any rational state. Thus, instead of capital being passed on directly to the son, it would revert at death to some permanent social administration, which would presumably entrust it for productive use to those of the members who were acquitting themselves the most effectively in business.

HABITS OF CONDUCT

Competition.

Next to private property, the feature to which most exception seems to have been taken in the present system is the habit of conduct: " competition." This, however, is also the feature which until recent years has been most highly lauded by the majority engaged in industry. It has been regarded not only as a valuable stimulant to business, but also as a means of protecting the customer against the exploitation of producers. Even in present times, business men find themselves commending competition and then condemning it again in the same breath. Judgments seem to vacillate according to the inspiration of the moment; and there is no criterion capable of showing what ultimate position should be held.

Whence arises the confusion? One element in it, at least, would seem to be that the word "competition" is employed to cover two distinct meanings. In the first place, there is the *act* of competition, which is the bare process by which one person or unit is measured against another. And, secondly, there is the *spirit* of competition, which denotes the attitude of the subjects being measured. Men may compete with each other, in the sense of putting forth their utmost effort in order that they may be tested and compared, without evincing any spirit whatever of rivalry or jealousy; and to confound this act of competition with the spirit of competition is to obscure the issue at the outset.

Acts of competition, whether they be good or bad, are indispensable in any régime. Quite evidently, it would be impossible to make the necessary selection of the most efficient men for the most delicate work, or to determine which are the weakest units to be removed from the business field, or, in general, to secure the square peg for the square hole throughout industry, unless there were some method of measuring men and institutions against each other. Acts of competition, in one form or another, must be a day-by-day occurrence.

Morally, the effect of these acts can depend only on the spirit in which they are approached. The measurement of one person against another cannot of itself have the least moral significance; for if neither were to be informed of the result, the act would be equivalent to that of comparing the horse-power of two engines. It is the effect on the persons when they learn the result that matters. And this effect must in turn depend essentially on the " tone " or spirit in which they compete.

If men enter the competition in the spirit of self-interest, coveting for themselves the fruits of the competition, inevitably there will be some sour grapes in the harvest. There will always be a winner and a loser. And the loser will be embittered. Moreover, since all standards of business achievement are relative, to be great one must be greater than one's neighbours; and the proof of greatness can only be given through some form of comparative measurement. Competition is thus seized upon by the self-ambitious as a means of demonstrating their superiority over others. When thus engaged in, its results are doubly regrettable : those who gain in the comparison become still more obsessed with their own magnificence; those who lose become soured and more despondent.

It cannot be said that the spirit of competition is

extremely intense in Great Britain at the present time; its people are not unphilosophical. There are many who enter competition because there is no escape from it, rather than out of any personal zest. And where-ever the motive behind the competition is thus virtually neutral there can be no serious moral by-product from it.

In ideal conditions, where the common motive becomes that of " contribution," competition would be accepted in its true light merely as a means of sorting individuals into the positions for which they are most suited, and of securing the removal of the least efficient business units. Since the desire of all members of society would be to see their common purposes attained in the highest degree, the need for distributing functions in accordance with capacity would be recognised by all; they would regard the results of competitive measurement as absolutely and impersonally good, whatever its effect upon their own careers.

Apart entirely from these ethical considerations there is a purely economic aspect of the problem of competition : the aspect which relates primarily to business efficiency and to the attainment of maximum output. Of necessity the economic issues arising out of competition must be considered in any study of the good and the bad in the present system; but it is to be noted that, as a rule, they tend to find their solution through the efforts of those within industry acting in their own interests, irrespective of any moral considerations. This is especially so in the case of competitive waste, in which the expenses of advertising, the overlapping of administration and marketing, the concealment of trade information, and dealing in small quantities are drawbacks to be weighed against possible advantages from the stimulus which fierce competition may give. This problem of competitive waste does not appear to admit of the same solution for all industries. Rather, each industry must be tested on its own merits, to determine whether it is likely to give greater advantages under decentralised, competitive control, as in the case, say, of tailoring, or whether it would produce better results under a single control, as in the case of the postal service. As noted, the various industries are tending to find their own solution according to their special situation. At the present time the tendency is steadily in the direction of centralisation and the cutting out of competition, a movement which does not seem by any means to have run its course as yet.

What is quite beyond question, however, is that no matter how far the movement for the suppression of competition goes, there will remain at all times some form of competitive measurement, if only to secure a sound distribution of talent throughout industry; and that, secondly, the moral consequences of this form of competition will depend essentially upon the motive of those engaging in it.

Economic Groups and Divisions.

Attention may now be turned on a further " habit
of conduct " which, of all features of the system, raises
the most complex moral and economic problems:
" the employment of one group by another." It would
seem to be almost a presumption, perhaps, to treat
this subject in a few pages. But there are certain
exigencies,[1] and the attempt must be made to deal as
compactly as may be with the complexities of the
subject.

Let us note at the outset certain fundamental conditions which emerge as the result of " the employment of one group by another "—conditions which
render this habit so peculiarly productive of unrest.

The habit, first of all, severs the community into
two groups. This, however, is not *of itself* necessarily
a factor of disturbance, since the division is on the
basis of economic function, and does not therefore
carry with it any implication of superiority or
inferiority, as does a division into social grades.

The central cause which renders this grouping into
employers and employed so inherently inflammable is
that the relationship between them is founded on a very
special form of contract. It is a contract which, since
it affects wages, is for either side vitally important.
The one party to the contract sells his labour—substantially everything he possesses—in return for his

---

[1] A pamphlet such as this, containing in essence only one idea, should be
as short as is reasonably possible.

F

entire livelihood. The other buys the labour at a price—a price which determines whether his business will remain profitable. Thus, if either party loses at all in the bargain, the loss is serious, and the dissatisfaction intense.

A further element aggravating the position is that this wage contract, as a rule, is of a makeshift, provisional character. It is usually the result of a trial of bargaining strength by the two parties; and since there are wide variations in the power which either of them can bring to bear, the one being dominant at one time and the other at another, the bargains effected are almost invariably regarded by one side as unsatisfactory, and hence to be readjusted as soon as it is able to renew its strength. The relationship between the two groups is in consequence most unstable; and, by reason of the immensity of the stakes involved for both sides, it is liable to produce a conflagration at any time.

In the majority of cases, it is for the workers that the contract proves most unsatisfactory. Their stake, individually, is greater. Their reserves are relatively small. And, as statistics of the outcome of strikes reveal, they are most frequently the losers. But, however poor the contract from the point of view of the worker, he is often in the position (especially in Great Britain) of being unable to afford to terminate it. If not assured of work elsewhere, he cannot, individually, risk losing the existing contract. This

may place him in the position of being compelled to
accept what seems unjust; and in many other ways it
may put him at the mercy of his particular employer.
Here and there it is unquestionable that this position
has been presumed upon. The sword of Damocles, in
the form of threatened dismissal, has been held over
the head of the worker as a means of exacting not
merely effort, but servility. It is this feature in the
situation which has at times raised the outcry against
" wage slavery."

The causes for this complaint are in various ways
steadily receding. But there is one circumstance
which renders it quite impossible (in the existing
economic order—uncorrected by any system of
voluntary redistribution of income) for the workers as
a whole to secure contracts which will give them final
satisfaction. And here we reach the very crux of the
problem of industrial relations. By virtue of the
economic position of the employing group, the income
of this group is protected so that it will *always* form a
high proportion of the national income. No matter
what the workers may do, or by what process wages are
fixed, the wage-earning group cannot be caused to
gain materially at the expense of employers and
owners. The position of the non-wage-earning group
is virtually impregnable.

This is a point which needs some developing, though
it will be impossible here to do more than hint at the
reasoning which underlies the statement. The state-

ment, itself, broadly, is that it is peculiarly difficult for employers and workers to reach final agreement, because it is not possible, and never will be possible under the existing order, for workers to secure wages which will even approach to equality with the average return to employers. The owning and employing group in general receive Rent for their land, Interest on capital owned, and Profit as the return for their relative efficiency in business. These three classes of income have for as far back as statistics reach (more than fifty years) together amounted to almost half the total national income; and in spite of every effort of labour organisations, this share has remained substantially unaltered.

Profits are perhaps less effectively protected than the other forms of income; but even in this case there is a limit to the extent to which wages can encroach on them. For if wages are forced up at the expense of profits, the blow falls most heavily on the weaker firms in the industry, some of which will be driven into bankruptcy. The wage-earners can thus only attack the profits of the stronger section of the industry by crumbling up the weaker end. This is a process injurious to the workers themselves, since it causes dislocation and unemployment, and it obliges them to desist at an early stage. The profits of the stronger group are thus protected by a buffer, as it were, of weaker firms.

Whatever shields profits also shields Interest.

Every firm must pay the interest due to persons who have lent money to it—holders of its debentures and preference shares—before a penny of profit can be drawn by those who own and direct the enterprise. Hence, in the case of any firm in which profit has been protected sufficiently to leave but one penny of it, the interest on borrowed capital will have been *wholly* protected. All the interest must have been paid. But there is a further safeguard for interest. Whenever a person investing money is liable to lose a part of it, he demands and receives a higher rate on his loan. There is added to the ordinary rate of interest an "insurance margin," an extra percentage varying according to the risk of loss. Hence, if in any industry wage-earners were to succeed in seriously endangering profits and interest, no lenders would subsequently invest money in the industry except at a rate high enough to offset the risk.

As regards Rent, this is paid by a firm as a prior charge even to interest. Rent is a payment made actually as a condition of the right to continue occupying premises or exploiting land; and there is thus less prospect of drawing on rent to increase wages than there is of securing profit or interest.

The total effect of these defences for profit, interest, and rent is, as shown by the figures, that in spite of the growth of trade unions and their unremitting assaults on the income of the employing group, this group, small as it is, has succeeded in retaining nearly half the national income throughout.[1] And although trade unions may have caused an increase of wages in the *absolute* sense, they have not improved their situation relatively to that of the employing group; neither have they reduced the extreme disparities in individual incomes.

This failure remains so obvious to the eye in both city and country that it scarcely requires statistical support. And, because it is so evident, there can be little prospect that trade union leaders will at any future time be finally satisfied with the kind of wage-bargain they are able to make at present. They may be fully convinced of the abortiveness of their past attempts and, intellectually, little sanguine as to success of future efforts to reduce the inequalities of incomes; notwithstanding, they will never in practice accept the present situation as final, but will continue to attempt the impossible.

If a situation permanently satisfying to both sides is to be reached under the present economic system, it can only be through some magnanimity on the part of the employers' group—through some move whereby the employers surrender a part of their specially protected income *voluntarily*. Since the employers as a body are in a position of peculiar strength, and

---

[1] Rent, Interest and Profit have together ranged from about 41 to 50 per cent. of the National Income. See *International Labour Review*, July 1927.

In Great Britain the employed outnumbers the employer group by approximately 24 to 1 (Census of 1921). In the United States, with a more widely spread population and much agriculture, the proportion is considerably smaller.

receive the lion's share of the national income, it is only from them that any considerable increase of liberality is possible; and the onus of the solution rests primarily, though perhaps not entirely, upon them.

This is broadly the position as it stands at present. The masses of the workers receive individually a return which is frequently not a tithe of that which is received and spent by the employers and owners. And the employer-owner group in general, apart from distinguished exceptions, do not appear prepared to make further concessions towards equality.

With this situation as the general background of discussion, we may proceed to consider what would be the effect on industrial relations of a progressive change of attitude on the part of the dominant group.   To this end various degrees of motives, ranging from extreme "self-interest" to that of "contribution," will be assumed as operating in the stronger group and in industry generally; and the attempt will be made to trace the concrete result of each upon the relationship between the groups.

It is apparent, without any consideration of the details of causation, that strikes and lockouts must be more numerous in proportion to the intensity of self-interest.   When there is only one total product to be shared, and two groups to share it, the more unscrupulous either side is in gaining its maximum, the more relentless will be the struggle between them. There is no question that many complicating factors enter to increase the difficulty of securing agreement; but, at bottom, it is self-interest which is the real cause forcing the two parties into conflict; and only as this motive is progressively curbed can there be any prospect of an abatement of strife.

A first step towards improvement will be possible when self-interest is sufficiently under control to allow of the frank interchange of information. When there is full publicity with regard to the current profitableness and prospects of industries, this at least will provide the ground of fact on which reason can lay its foundations.

The next stage involves a willingness to negotiate on the basis of the facts and to set up joint machinery to that end; and, in the event of failure to reach a compromise through this joint machinery, an undertaking by both sides to refer the dispute to some impartial body.

These suggestions for the renunciation of the intensely acquisitive attitude, and the acceptance of recourse to reason, are now a matter of commonplace; and progress towards their adoption is fairly rapid. But they would not seem sufficient alone to end strife. The one basic difficulty which confronts any proposal for the peaceful settlement of wage disputes remains still unremoved; namely, that, under the existing economic order, in which a large proportion of the total national income is ear-marked for rent, interest, or profits, *no* system of wage-adjustment, no matter how peaceful or how cleverly devised, can succeed in giving to the wage-earners what they can regard as a satisfying share of the national income. Whether wages are fixed by trial of strength, or by negotiated compromise, or by arbitral award, it is impossible in any case to raise the wage-earners' share *as a whole* materially in relation to that of the employer-owner group as a whole. Thus, even if a comprehensive system of wage-arbitration were to be introduced and supported by all the goodwill in the industrial universe, it would have little prospect of surviving. For as soon as it was found that the new system of settlement could place the workers as a whole in no better relative position than they held before, it would be subject to attack, especially by those bodies which felt they might secure for themselves a better bargain by direct action than they gained through arbitration. And, sooner or later, the system would crumble.

Hence, we are thrown back again on the conclusion that, as an accompaniment, and a reinforcement, to any scheme of wage-arbitration, there must be some further *voluntary* sacrifice by the employer-owner group of their protected gains. By one process or another of arbitrary renunciation, a redistribution of wealth must be effected so that the present extremes of income may become less glaring. So long as these extremes remain, any system of wage-arbitration which, in a weak moment, the workers have been induced to accept, must ultimately appear a hoax.

The possible methods of redistribution are already known, and are for the most part already in operation here and there by enlightened employers. One way of increasing the income of wage-earners is through ownership-sharing. As already noted, if in any given industry a flat rate of wages is applied throughout, it is impossible to raise that rate beyond a certain limit owing to its breaking up the weaker end of the industry too rapidly. This wage limit still allows, however, of considerable profit amongst the more efficient units—a profit which the wage-earners cannot directly touch. But if all the employers in the firms making more than a certain percentage of profit were to say to their employees—" We are unable to raise your wages *as such*, since the standard rate must apply to the whole industry; but we will make you co-owners of our capital, so that you may receive interest, and we will make you co-owners of our enterprise, so that you may share in our variable profits "—this would make a material difference to the relative incomes of the employing and employed groups. Co-ownership, if extensively developed, would go far toward evening up the existing inequalities of income. And both directly and indirectly it would create the right atmosphere for the peaceful settlement of all disputes between employers and employed.

Another method of redistribution attainable through the further evolution of industrial motive and social outlook, is that of increasing taxation for expenditure on social services. This method, again, is considerably advanced already; but in its completely matured form it signifies that through the machinery of the State the fullest opportunity for personal development will be afforded to the wage-earner and to his children, in so far as this can be effectively guaranteed by Government action. The method involves, to be effective, the cutting down of the personal consumption of the employer-owner group, concurrently with the increase of taxation, and the application of the extra revenue to such services as the extension of education, the improvement of hygiene, housing, and general municipal conditions.

It should be emphasised, however, that taxation is valueless as a method of redistributing wealth unless it is accompanied by a reduction in the taxpayer's personal consumption. Taxes may be paid either out of savings or out of income ordinarily applied to personal uses. If they are paid out of savings, they tend to check the growth of industry, and thus cause restraints which may more than offset the gain from the spread of income. The disadvantage can be avoided only if taxpayers, when a new tax is imposed, reduce their personal spending by the amount of the tax. This obviously involves no small degree of altruism. Hence the conclusion is again reached that the one fundamental requirement for securing a more even distribution of income is *voluntary* sacrifice on the part of those who own.

The final result reached here as regards the habit "employment of one group by another" may be stated briefly in this way. The main cause of friction between the two groups is the inequality in the distribution of income. Whereas the group which is employed outnumbers many times that which owns and employs, it receives only a slightly greater share of the national income. Moreover, by no ingenuity is it possible to invent a system of wage-adjustment which will materially lessen the resulting personal inequalities. Schemes of arbitration and conciliation provide only the means of making the best of a situation they cannot cure. The only ways in which greater equality of income might be achieved, apart from direct gifts and the pooling of income, are, first, through profit- and ownership-sharing and, secondly, through taxation. Both these methods involve, for their effectiveness, the subjection of the acquisitive motive. They can be made to succeed only if tax-payers and those who wish to share what they possess are willing to restrain their personal consumption; and this involves a new motive to impose discipline on the old.

Other Features of the Behaviour of the System.

This discussion of "habits of conduct," whilst having covered the two most significant of such habits, cannot be without numerous gaps. It is manifestly impossible to examine each one of the

innumerable business customs which fall within this
category, and test it to see wherein it is good and
bad, and why. However, the reader might perhaps
aid the completion of the process. Almost every
person who has the least contact with industry has
found himself particularly repelled by one or more of
its " habits of conduct." It may be some form of
business organisation, some method of selling or
advertising, some principle of trade unionism, some
method of paying wages, or other habit; but whatever the habit may be which gives offence, the injured
person might examine it in the attempt to affirm or
refute this contention : that all adverse conditions in
the present system are due, either to some unfruitful
habits which have *emerged* because we are self-
interested, or to potentially useful habits which are
abused because we are self-interested.

Habits in the Use of Economic Mechanism

A survey of the good and the bad in the present
system would be seriously incomplete if some attention
were not given to certain of the ingenious devices and
instruments which have been evolved for smoothing
the way of production. Amongst these, as noted
earlier, the chief instrument in use is money. Were
this medium not available for easing the exchange of
goods, trade on a large scale would seem inconceivable.
Society would be reduced to a system of barter, the
exchange of cloth for cattle, trinkets for bread, wine

for leather, each would-be barterer being compelled
to hawk his wares around until by some lucky coincidence he, as, say, producer of food desiring fuel
should chance upon some producer of fuel desiring
food, and then be able to effect a satisfactory bargain.
Money displaces this clumsy procedure.

But it does more than this : it enables every producer and consumer to find the best market. Under
barter, any man whose need is very great, and who
has difficulty in striking just that coincidence of wants
which will enable him to exchange his wares, must
be seriously at a disadvantage in bargaining; he
must be very much at the mercy of one whose need
is less or who can simulate indifference. When, however, all goods are bought with money, the would-be
purchaser is no longer dependent on a chance coincidence; he possesses an instrument which he can
change at any place and for anything he wants; he
can buy therefore from any one of a large number of
producers and, in fact, compel them to compete for
his custom. Money thus permits the purchaser to
find the most advantageous offer. It may be regarded
as not merely a convenience, but as a powerful
instrument of justice.

This instrument is, however, indispensable even as
a convenience. It would be difficult, in fact, to
conceive of any form of civilisation without money
or some corresponding medium of exchange. Even
in a state where all distribution was effected through

the central administration, ration tickets would be
required to take the place of currency, and indent
forms for raw materials and machinery would have
to be used by industry instead of cheques. These
substitutes would be little else than rather inefficient
types of money; that is, they would perform certain
of the functions of money without yielding all its
advantages.

One advantage which only money can give is that
it creates the price system; and the price system, in
turn, provides a unique service. In general, the price
which is placed on an article corresponds fairly closely
to the cost of producing the article. The more labour
and capital there is involved in its production, the
higher, as a rule, will be the price. This means that
when a buyer is adjusting his purchases so as to gain
the greatest satisfaction *with due regard to the prices
of the articles*, what he is doing in reality is to take
into account *the labour and capital involved in their
production*. Since this effect is universal, the community as a whole is enabled to spread its purchases
in such a way as to gain the greatest satisfaction from
its available supply of labour and capital. Otherwise
expressed, it is through the price system that the
community's labour and capital are called into play
in such proportions and along such channels as to
yield the highest attainable total of satisfaction.

This is possible only through a price system, or
through a price system by another name. Under a

scheme of rationing by the State, for instance, the amounts of any articles produced and distributed would have to be determined arbitrarily by the administration. And unless there were gross waste of any particular item there would be no means of checking the judgment of the administration. It is true that the community might be allowed to express some option by being presented with ration tickets valid for a given quantity of particular supplies; but this in reality would be equivalent to allowing them money. And if the articles distributed were differentiated according to their cost of production, this, again, would be equivalent to pricing them. Some form of price system is, in fact, indispensable to any scientific method of distributing goods.

Closely associated with the price system is the profit system. When the price is fixed for any industry more or less equal to the costs of production of the last firms needed in the industry, profit will accrue to the more efficient firms in proportion to their capacity to reduce costs below the price so fixed. Profit is, in fact, the reward for *relative* efficiency. But the profit system is not merely the means through which efficient management is recompensed : it provides, in addition, the means for rooting out the inefficient. The capacity to make profit, or at least to avoid loss, is the determinant of a man's remaining in business. If he cannot pass this test, he must make way for others.

The profit test may not be a perfect one; but there is no escape from the necessity of some such test. If industry is to remain dynamic there must be some means of comparing units with each other and causing the more feeble to retire. Whether any system other than that of profit could be devised seems doubtful. The basis of any criterion of efficiency must clearly be the capacity to keep expenses low. But any accountancy system which is capable of measuring this capacity must be fundamentally the same as that which yields the profit and loss account in present times. It would have to show in detail all the expenses of the unit and subtract them from receipts—the resultant being what we now call profit.

In this connection it may be shown that the wages system, or something equivalent to it, is also indispensable if there is to be any test set up of the efficiency of different units. Many of the expenses of production which must be measured for this purpose are the expenses of labour or services. But since one labourer can produce more than another, a skilled workman delivering twice as much work as an apprentice, and an expert manager saving ten times as much on costs as a novice, there must be some means of assessing the productive value of each labourer or employee, in order to be able to compare the efficiency of any two business directorates. The wages system has this effect of placing a price upon each person's labour roughly according to the amount he can pro-

G

duce. In present times the adjustment is much disturbed; but it suffices at least to permit the comparison of firms in the same industry and to secure the weeding out of the least efficient. Without the wages system some other method would have to be devised for showing the relative productive capacity of employees, or, otherwise expressed, for fixing the cost of different types of labour. To discover such a means which is not the virtual equivalent of the wages system would indeed tax the imagination.

Each of the economic mechanisms described above yields its own peculiar advantage to society. The first, money, is invaluable as a means of securing the exchange of goods. The second, the price system, ensures that goods will be produced in such proportions that the community as a whole gains the maximum satisfaction attainable from its available labour and capital. The profit system provides a means of eliminating the decadent part of an industry and, although incapable alone of raising the most efficient personnel to the top, is a factor tending towards this end. In this it is aided by the wages system, which permits the assessment of the cost of different types of labour, and so renders accurate accounting possible.

All four systems are closely related to one another. If money were to be removed, the three remaining systems would disappear with it, together with the

specific advantages they yield. If the wages system
were to be abolished, the price system would lose
much of its usefulness; for there would be no method
of determining the true cost of production of articles,
and the prices would have to be arbitrarily fixed by
the state. Hence, if the desire is felt to remove any
one of these mechanisms, it may mean removing, or
at least dislocating, all the rest. And any economic
system which is suggested as an alternative for the
present must either retain these four mechanisms *in
toto*, or else introduce a completely new set which will
not only perform the same functions individually as
the present money, price, profit and wages systems,
but will also " hold together " with the same degree
of perfection as the present mechanisms.

But why wish to change them in any case? They
are at the most only instruments. As such, they
may be applied ill or well, according to the motive
of those using them. Money, for instance, if used
for the purposes for which it was initially created, is
the greatest material boon to society. If it has subsequently become the tool of gamblers, or is erected
as a god by others, this is a condemnation not of
money, but of those abusing it. Again, the price
system cannot be cast aside merely because, here
and there, it is wrenched and juggled with by pools
and speculators. And profits, no matter how great
they are, cannot of themselves lead to evil. In fact,
the greater the profits, the better it would be—

provided that they were devoted by the recipients to the service of the community. If the motive inspiring the business owner were to create income for the promotion of research, and schools, and works of beauty, no possible complaint could arise from the magnitude of his profits.

Hence, no matter how numerous and revolting the false uses may be which the present imperfect society has found for its economic mechanisms, it would be against all the dictates of rationality to exclude these mechanisms from the scheme of a model economic system unless something technically superior to them can be found.

* * * * *

The chief conclusion from these reflections on the good and the bad in the present system—the conclusion which for us shows the focal point for all efforts of economic reconstruction—is that there is one outstanding feature which vitiates the system in its entirety : namely, the motive. It is the motive of self-interest which, lying at the basis of every act in industry, and determining either the character or the mode of use of its instruments and habits, has cast a blemish over all branches of the system.

At the outset it was possible to show that the motive itself, when carried to an extreme, fails completely to satisfy the accepted test of " harmony." By its very nature, extreme self-interest involves a struggle amongst individuals to acquire a large share

of a limited common fund of goods, to force themselves
above others, and to attain liberties which trench
upon the liberties of others. Self-interest inevitably
throws men into conflict with each other. But, apart
from this, the same motive permeates and infects all
other branches of the system. It is at once the main
cause of the existence and the main cause of the abuse
of the "right of private property." Property in
private hands, if adapted to its special, more symbolic
uses, may be a means of creating certain new qualities
in life. It may give variety and greater depth to the
power of self-expression. And it may make possible
high art in men's exchanges. On the other hand,
property may be vulgarised; measured in terms of
money; amassed; vaunted; and made the basis of
class distinctions. All depends upon the purposes
inspiring those who acquire and use the property.

Similarly, the good and bad in competition are
dependent essentially on the motives of the competitors. "Acts of competition" themselves are
necessary in any dynamic state; they are the means
of securing the survival of the fit. But whether these
acts will produce craftiness and friction, or whether
they will be met with the Stoic indifference of an
Epictetus, must depend primarily on the attitude of
the competitors.

"The employment of one group by another" is a
habit especially liable to produce sore places in industrial relations. Here again, however, if the search for

causes is pressed far enough back, it will be found that self-interest is at bottom the real source of irritation. It is this which makes men conceal their gains, refuse to compromise, and grasp and retain the limit of what the economic system permits them. And it is this intense acquisitiveness which blocks the way to any .serious movement for harmony in industry.

Finally, the influence of the motive is shown most clearly in the use of the instruments of industry. Under its influence money, a perfect instrument for its own intended purposes, either becomes grotesquely deified as an end in itself, or is profaned for speculation. The profit system, also a valuable economic instrument itself, becomes the breeding-ground of profiteers and leads to gross extravagance. In each case, however, it is not the instrument at fault, but the fact that it becomes the tool of exploitation. And the remedy, if any, rests not in the removal of the instrument, but in the attack on the earthiness of human outlook.

In brief, it is upon the development of some new motive in industry that depends any future prospect of securing a more satisfying system.

CHAPTER IV

INDUSTRIAL MOTIVE

ACHIEVEMENT in matters of conduct seems to involve, in almost all instances, the attainment of some form of balance. Generosity most often consists in giving without destroying the power to give again. The highest affection is in loving a few intensely, whilst not forgetting the unfriended many. True philosophy is to perceive the abstract and the profound without losing touch with human detail. In all things the position of poise seems to be the most nearly faultless; and it is the search for this position which is the mark of conscious striving towards the good.

Such a belief is perhaps not universally true, since in matters of life and death men are not concerned with finding a balance. It nevertheless has much force in the sphere of industrial motive, now to be considered. In the discussion just closed all findings converged on the belief that it is self-interest, nót in its first expression, but in its excess, which throws friction into the system. Further, it was urged that in the attempt to form some new system the chief step needed would be to search for, and to educate and develop, new motive. The theme now before us is that, whatever the new motive found may be, it will not be able, independently, to build a more satisfying economic scheme than self-interest has done. Only a balance of motives can achieve this. The full measure of satisfaction can be drawn from the economic system only when self-interest transfuses with, and is held and modulated by other-interest, the two motives forming jointly the basis of the system. Were these motives separated and pressed to their extremes, they would seem to end, the one in chaos, the other in unsubstantiality.

In order to show the grounds for this view it would not seem necessary to draw examples from, or reason on the basis of the economic system itself. The reasoning may be founded on the relationships between men and groups in all spheres, the same thoughts and findings being applicable to the field of industry as to that of the wider life. Hence we may now leave the purely economic sphere and examine the question of motive in relation to men's action in whatever course or condition it may be found. At a later stage, in Chapter VI, it will be possible again to give attention to the economic system specifically, and apply the results drawn from this chapter to show how far some fresh motive, or joint motives, may reinvigorate the system.

The aim at this stage, then, is to examine each form of self-interest separately to find how completely it or its opposite would lead to futility if the two were not joined. Thus if the opposite of " natural " self-interest may be said to be " imaginative " other-interest, it will be necessary to discuss here to what extent these two must be combined to produce their golden mean. " Acquired " self-interest will, in the same way, have to be considered in relation to " acquired " other-interest; and " group " self-interest, or interest in the family, in relation to interest in the world community.

Natural Self-Interest.

As has been seen, one source from which " natural " self-interest arises is the same as that which creates the power to see things physically beautiful. To be self-interested by nature is to seek appeasement for the hunger and sex urges and to desire play for the senses of touch, sight, scent, hearing, or taste. When thus framed in crude terms, " natural " self-interest may seem to imply earthiness rather than exhilaration, and may be linked in the mind with anathemas against fleshly sins. In truth, this " natural " self-interest, when most natural, is simply the unspoiled passion to enjoy. It means exultation in the things of Nature, the sea, the open country—everything, in-deed, spread for enrichment. All light, warmth, and coolness; sound, quietude, and music; motion, stillness, freshness; are gifts breathed in through the senses. To be interested in this everything is to have that " natural " self-interest without which life would be hollow.

In its earliest beginnings " natural " self-interest is thus a form of primal good which lies at the basis of much other good. It is the root of all feeling, and therefore of enjoyment and of the power to give enjoyment. If it leads in the end, when given rein, to things which injure, this can only be through its excess, and not its use. As in the case of all other evil, the evil from it is but " unprotected " good— unprotected or, in this case, unhusbanded and unrestrained.

Good may be said to consist partly in a thing's intrinsic worth, partly in the power to give it rarity or refinement. Things which are used with due feeling for their sensitiveness or intimacy gain value. Things held with clumsy hands seem to suffer pros- titution. Thus, in the case of that good which arises from self-interest the gain must be in proportion as due restraint is imposed on the motive to consume. To grasp unsparingly all pleasures within reach, or hoard them as a miser, is to destroy. For beauty lies flimsily on life, and recoils when clutched.

There can be no escape, then, from progressive loss of satisfaction as self-interest is driven beyond its first crest of value. Viewed hedonistically, the aim of self-interest may be said to be that of making sense pleasure a maximum. The one way in which this aim may be secured is not, however, through directly gratifying the senses, but through increased tone reached through restrained diet and discipline. It is these which yield what the epicure desires. And it is to dwell in a fool's paradise to imagine that the end can be attained by a lavish feeding of the senses; to pander to them or build cushions round them is ultimately to enfeeble; and although in the actual process there may appear to be some gain, the final state will be less pleasing than the first. There is in this process, moreover, the supreme risk of enslaving the subject to his acquired tastes, causing him to enter the vicious circle in which each indulgence leads to more craving and in which the only known satisfaction is relief from appetite.

If, then, it is evident that "natural" self-interest must in the extreme mean loss even to the individual who gives rein to it, leading him past freshness, the need is to find some means of placing a restraint upon the motive at the point at which it gives high value. The paradox must be accepted that the æsthetic life is possible only to those who are in some degree ascetic, and that a balance must be achieved by placing upon the urges which crave direct satisfaction a discipline which will keep the satisfaction fresh.

The discipline needed is obviously to be sought through some opposite motive : a motive such as that described earlier as "imaginative other-interest." This implies, where things physical are concerned, first, the power to feel the value of these things;

secondly, the power, through imagination, to feel satisfaction when others reap the value. Exactly how the satisfaction is gained, or through what mind process, is a question on which all may wrangle; but that it exists as something native will seem clear to anyone who has seen, for instance, a child presiding over a doll's tea-party; and that it requires imagination needs no proof.

Where this other-interest exists it must have two effects. First it must cause the individual to restrain his own use of material things and impose asceticism on him to some extent. Secondly, it must lead to the wide spreading among those who need them most of the materials thus saved. Inevitably it means multiplying the satisfaction on both sides.

The main thought to be stressed here, however, is that, satisfying though this " imaginative other-interest " may be as a motive, it can be of no value independently. It may lead to a large contributive-ness; it may produce wider satisfaction; or it may create universal social warmth; but it can achieve these things only in association with its counterpart " self-interest." Alone, " other-interest " would pro-duce a vacuum. If all were anxious that others should enjoy, and had no appetite to enjoy themselves, give and take would lose meaning. In order that some may give, others must be anxious to receive; and this implies self-interest.

There must be developed, therefore, a certain

partnership between self-interest and other-interest. A balance of the two motives is needed, such that from self-interest is drawn the power to appreciate the good which comes from experiences recorded through the senses, and, from other-interest, imagination sufficient to allow the same good to be realised when it is experienced by others. The one gives knowledge of the worth-whileness of the experience itself; the other the urge to see it spread.

" Acquired " Self-Interest.

A similar balance would seem needed between self-interest and other-interest of the " acquired " type. Assuming that personalities individually have a transcendent value, each meriting separate interest, there arises the need for attaining a poised sense of the value of one individual in relation to all others. Each may have meaning and value independently; but the significance of each is enlarged by reaction with, and through the recognition of the significance of, other individuals. There is a mutuality and an importance-relationship between one individual and the wider group, a balanced consciousness of which would be a chief aim of self-education.

The special mark of " acquired " self-interest, it was said, is a tendency towards prepossession in self *qua* end. It is an acquired mental state which gives rise to a prior interest in the one personality. Its effect, socially, is to create anxiety for position, or for prominence, or for any forms of acquisition which may seem distinctive. In industry its expression is rather in the urge to find lucrative work with a view to status. It creates both the fear of unemployment and the desire for better employment. In all cases it signifies in the mind a concern not to lose caste or to rise to a higher caste, this aim involving usually the service of the single individual as an end.

The extreme case of " acquired " self-interest is when an individual regards himself as more significant than all others as an end. Irrational though this may seem when considered objectively, it may represent a state that is fairly widespread. Indeed, the reason for its escaping indictment as irrational is perhaps precisely that it is so widespread. When all regard themselves as more important than the rest, although it is impossible for more than one to be right, the outlook of all is thought reasonable.

Introspection will, no doubt, show that few of us are able to escape from this strangeness entirely. The experience is common, for instance, that when complimented on an achievement, we feel warmed and gratified. If another is complimented on the same achievement, we are unmoved. Our minds are not on the achievement, but on ourselves. Again, if it is our blunder which jeopardises a scheme, we lose sleep. If another commits the blunder, we lose no sleep. The concern is not for the damage, but for our personal standing. It is this obsession, this

" acquired " interest in self, that grips us. And the
fact that it is an obsession is shown from our ability,
occasionally, to step aside and see ourselves with the
reasonable eyes of humour.

If some change may be hoped from education, it
must be admitted by those of us who teach that so
far our methods have tended rather to increase the
obsession than remove it. This may be shown perhaps
from the process through which it emerges. In a
description given earlier it was shown that " acquired "
self-interest has at least some foundation in conditions
that are " natural." Each individual, as an infant,
becomes aware of himself very soon and very forcibly.
He learns to distinguish himself as an entity, separate
from other people. In the first months the whole of
his life is woven around things experienced in his own
body : hunger, irritation, pleasant things which
attract, and unpleasant things which have to be
fought against. The infant becomes, in fact, much
more keenly conscious of himself than of other
persons, and naturally begins by regarding himself
as of greater importance than all others.

As soon as mind begins to strengthen, however,
there arises the possibility of experiencing through
imagination the feelings of others, and thus of developing a true awareness or appreciation of their importance. The growth of a " consciousness of others " may,
with the aid of education, begin just as soon as a child
is capable of " taking notice." But whether it will, in

fact, emerge, or whether consciousness of self will continue to predominate, must depend almost entirely on early training. In the educational environment with which most are surrounded to-day, the strengthening of the consciousness of self is favoured, so that it develops as a rule into a greater or less degree of self-importance.

In the home the child's life continues to be built around his own likes and dislikes, and it is not until years are well advanced, if then, that he is expected to concern himself actively with the wants of others. He is constantly demanding and acquiring, and is rarely ministering even in a minor way. Self is allowed to occupy almost all thought.

Later, in games, he is expected to stand in his own corner and fend for himself; and he takes credit or discredit only for his own performance. Team games provide an exception, in that they do to a certain extent take the emphasis off the individual accomplishment and give encouragement to the idea of contributing. The opportunity to take part in sports of this nature represents, however, virtually the only regular opportunity open to adolescents for contributing to some achievement which is not exclusively their own.

During all the serious, impressive hours of education, the child is occupied solely with his own affairs. At school he is taught to stand quite alone. To help another is almost a crime; and to be aided by another

certainly is. Marks are awarded; and each pupil is
urged to become a miser, counting gains and hoarding
them, and being at no time allowed to add to another's
wealth. On the contrary, he is compelled to guard
his own jealously so that he may be compared and
contrasted with his fellows. As a rule the pupils do
succeed in defeating efforts to pigeon-hole them in
this way; the co-operative spirit remains only partly
quelled. Nevertheless, they have rarely opportunity
for joining openly in some massed achievement, and
the whole tendency of the training is towards extreme
self-concentration.

While this is continuing year by year, it is attended
by a running commentary of suggestion by the
parents. A boy is constantly urged to " get on,"
which, being interpreted, means to get on above his
neighbours and become prominent. The question is
always : " What are you going to *be,* son ? "—not :
" What are you going to *add ?* "

At the University things improve a little. The
competitive spirit is less intense; and a man is no
longer forcibly pitted against his fellows. But even
there he has little or no chance of adding to the
success of others. He works only for his own degree,
his own fellowship, or his own prize.

Twenty years, or a hundred thousand conscious
hours, of this kind of training, under which a developing individual is constantly turned in on himself and
his own attainment, can only be expected to fill a

H

mind with an intense self-obsession. If self has been the focus of all attention throughout the whole of this formative period, it is inevitable that the ultimate *idée fixe* must emerge that we, as ends, are far more important than all others.

There is no question that we do, the large majority of us, think this. Numerous habits show it, if we would frankly search them. Yet—what palpable absurdity—that an entire community can exist almost all of whom imagine they have a significance above the rest !

" *Acquired* " *Other-Interest.*

However irrational this condition may seem it would nevertheless be equalled in futility were every, person completely self-disinterested. When men have no anxiety on their own behalf, it is impossible for others to have anxiety or feel sympathy for them; if they neither want nor lack anything, nor feel self-concern, nor sense any importance in their own existence, then there is no way in which others can express interest in them; and a community so composed would become dead as regards real personal intercourse. The members might, it is true, find entertainment in one another as psychological studies; but their relationship would be of a thin, intellectual texture; there could be no warmth in it. The position would be akin to that which might be conceived as resulting from the universalising of the

Stoic doctrine : a position in which feeling is repressed
and self ignored so that everywhere there is a sense of
emotional blankness.[1]

" Other-interest " alone would thus seem as profit-
less as " self-interest." On the one hand, " self-
interest " if universalised would produce a condition
in which all persons, being concentrated solely upon
themselves, could not give personal thought to sustain
others. On the other hand, " other-interest " generalised would create a state in which none could receive,
since none would be concerned to receive, thought
sustenance. All would be sending-stations of goodwill, but none would have sets for receiving.

In order that full value and meaning may be given
to the two motives they must therefore be made to
co-operate by being blended. The nature of their
desired union cannot, however, be discovered by comparing the importance of one self relatively to others,
and then adjusting the balance of interest in one self
and others according to relative merit. There is no
way of measuring personal value, and therefore no
means of comparison. The one approach that would
seem helpful would be to seek how the significance of
one individual may be enlarged through its broadening
appreciation of the significance of others. For if it is

[1] This may not be regarded as a criticism of the Stoic creed or, indeed, of
the Christain emphasis on self-denial, if it is accepted that complete denial
of self is impossible apart from suicide, and that what these faiths urge is
that, in the present, when there is an overwhelming excess of self-interest,
it is imperative that extreme efforts should be made for the self-denying
state to be approached.

true that a personality gains through becoming sensitive to other personalities, then the enrichment of one involves increased interest in others. That is, self-interest involves other-interest.

The secret of the desired fusion may be said to rest in the spread of each individual's intuitive link with the feeling of others. The final personal aim is of the nature of a " cosmic consciousness," the faculty to touch into the feeling of every life unit which also has consciousness. When this is found, the individual lives and has self-realisation only through the realisation of all life. He remains self-interested; but has no sense of whole satisfaction except through the movement of the entire life symphony or span.[1]

At this point self-interest and other-interest become necessarily one.

" Group Self-Interest."

The Englishman's home is sometimes called his castle. It is perhaps an unhappy simile. A castle throws in the mind the silhouette of something solitary, set on a hill; a redoubt with gates barred and drawbridge up; and self-sufficient.

It has no means of co-operating; it hugs itself apart, and the few who are in it; and they, being shut in, must find themselves stifled, quarrelsome,

---

[1] Edward Carpenter, A. E. Krishnamurti and other poets in recent times seem to have felt their way into this understanding and are helpful guides.

and petty-minded, confined to gossip, with affections suffocating for lack of freedom.

A more pleasing simile would be that of a harbour: a place of breezes with its gate open to the sea; whose trade is to welcome all comers, and refit them, for the sea; to have its own quietude, yet keep touch with every other thing by the sea; in chief, to work for, and be a part of, the sea.

SUMMARY

Since the point now reached is the end of the preliminary analysis, the further discussions bearing rather on what may develop than on what is, it will be well to draw together here the findings of past chapters and relate them to the later pages.

In Chapter II the chief conclusion was that the economic system may most suitably be regarded as the "habits," or the associated conduct, of the individuals comprised in it, and that as such it is the direct product of the quality of the individuals. Any radical change in the system must depend upon the ability to evolve and make effective a scheme of personal education.

In Chapter III this belief was followed by the attempt to discover in what respect, or in what features, the system fails, and to deduce the nature of the change required in it. The conclusion was that the change needed is some modification of motive.

The present chapter has altered the emphasis partly by showing that what is imperative is not an absolute change, but a more adequate balance, or fusion, of motives. To secure the most satisfying economic system, self-interest must be preserved inevitably, but accompanied by a powerful other-interest. There exists, of course, a combination of motives now, but other-mindedness is submerged; and the present practical task is to give it life.

When the discussion is to be turned later on the possibility of practical action, it will be convenient to make a change in the use of terms in one respect. Where economic action is involved, other-interest, no matter what origin it may have, must result in " contribution." Whether it is the opposite of " natural " or of " acquired " or of " group " self-interest, its outward expression must be through the attempt to add to the common gain. Hence there will be no ambiguity if, in the pages below, all motives based on other-mindedness are grouped together and described as " contributive."

On this understanding the aim, re-stated, may be said to be that of evoking widely the contributive spirit. For such a purpose education is the one medium. There is a sense in which it would seem that any kind of education must be better than none, assuming that it has the effect of strengthening the mental faculty. If a balance of motives is needed, it is within the mind that the balance must be achieved.

The mind is required as the arbiter of conduct, and unless it has ascendancy over the body, each bodily urge which happens for the moment to be the strongest will flood the mind, overwhelm its other contents, and secure dominion. Hence, education, and still more education, if it does in fact give mental strengthening, is one urgent need.

If the educational programme is to be directed specifically towards the development of contribution, it will involve, however, not only a considerable departure from existing average methods of school training, but also some penetration into the later career. There are two main educational forces at present at work. One is the recognised process of adolescent education designed to prepare individuals for their tasks in the economic system. The other is the economic system itself. To make a change in one without a change in the other would be almost valueless. For it matters little what sound motives a person may take with him into industry, they may readily be shattered unless he is able to fortify himself against the prevailing philosophy of the system.

There is thus needed an educational system in two parts. The first part, to be touched upon in the chapter immediately following, must deal with adolescent education and the adjustment of school methods with a view to giving opportunity for contributing. The second part, dealt with later in Chapter VI, will be to effect a breach in the present economic system, and in the breach insert the embryo of a new system. Only in this way will it be possible to show a new philosophy in being, and throw up a bulwark against the educational pressure of the old.

CHAPTER V

THE EDUCATION OF MOTIVE

In the search for simplicity, writers on education have frequently opened with the discussion of *the* aim in view, it being believed that the whole span of education may be made to serve some single, simple end. Such a belief would seem misguided. For if education is " introduction to life," its purposes must become as varied as there are phases in life. It must be the approach to citizenship, to art, understanding, work; and not only be an approach to these things, but also comprise them within itself. There is a sense in which it may be misleading to speak of education as having aims at all, since this may encourage the thought that education is no more than a means to other ends. Preferably it is to be conceived as an activity which should end only at death, being itself part of purpose, and a thread drawn through the entire life pattern.

It may be regarded as a means to further ends only in the sense that education builds up more education, and that mature understanding, when reached, is a unifying creative force. It is the co-ordinating, power-yielding, strife-diminishing factor; and in this sense it is a means to innumerable other ends.

In this brief discussion interest will necessarily be limited to one aspect only of educational purpose. Hence there will be occasion throughout for hesitating in the offer of proposals, and for leaving these flexible and adjustable to the needs of aims other than that in view here.

The aim with which we are chiefly and inevitably concerned in this chapter is the development of " attitude." The problem is to discover how education may be made to give vitality to the will to contribute. Or, in other words, the " introduction to life " which is to be planned is one which will lead to self-realisation through performance and outpouring.

That this should be taken as the end of education, or of those parts of it which bear on the growth of will and purpose, has been urged earlier mainly for economic reasons. It has been shown that the rise of a more powerful productive system depends almost wholly upon the development in industry of a more balanced and comprehensive motive. And in order that such a development may take place its foundations must be laid from the beginning in the educational process. Whereas industry may at present somewhat weaken sound attitudes formed in earlier training, it is nevertheless dependent for its own future strengthening upon the increasing power of such attitudes and upon the schools and colleges which promote them.

Since it is clear that the quality and vigour of the industrial system can be derived only from its human forces, the institutions which train these forces play inescapably a high economic rôle, and bear a like responsibility. As a corollary of this it might reasonably be held that whatever may be the chief economic need should throughout be taken as the aim of education. In other words, if industry lacks most the stimulus of wide motive, it would be the educator's continuous aim to create such motive.

A form of reasoning along such lines does indeed follow from the findings of preceding chapters. But such reasoning does not, as we have just seen, seem fully adequate alone to justify the acceptance of some motive as the chief aim of education. This would imply the subordination of the whole activity of early life to the requirements of only a part of a subsequent phase; and it would tend to degrade the educational system into little more than a factory for contriving and supplying the needs of industry. Obviously education has more sensitive aims than this. It has both a wider and a more intimate rôle, and in itself is an intensely human concern. Its aims must be conceived first in terms of the life and expression of those for whom it has first care. Only in so far as the needs of the developing individual, most widely conceived, run parallel with the particular needs of industry, would it seem right to give the latter any special weight.

Thus although this study may have led in the first place to the belief that in order to give stronger life to the present economic system it is necessary to concentrate the forces of education and direct them to this end, yet when the time now comes to consider education itself, there is found to be something repellent in the thought of converting it into merely a mechanism for sustaining the economic system. There would be a want of sensitiveness, and an element of social fanaticism, in laying the grasp of authority on a child and moulding him, as a spare part is moulded for a machine, to fit exactly into the frame of some economic system. Rather the aim must be broader in its more distant aspect, and more human in its immediate concern. The immediate aim must be to give the individual that independence, grace and clear perception which will permit him to discover a true form of self-realisation. This is indispensable to his happiness. The second, more distant, purpose would be to create in the individual those qualities which will make for the wider harmony and constructiveness of society as a whole. These two aims may be consistent. If it may be said that the course of self-realisation which gives most lasting satisfaction is performance in society's interest, it follows that the happiness of the individual and society's interest coincide. In the search for one the other is sought.

The more distant aim of education suggested here is broad enough to embrace the specific requirement of industry. It implies the creation of a motive which, whilst satisfying the individual and the social body in its full movement, would add in the particular field of industry the desired new power. It would add that stimulus which is the emphatic need of the economic system. But although the satisfaction of this need is in itself important, it may, in spite of everything said heretofore, be considered secondary, the essential grounds for taking " contribution " as the aim of motive-education being its personal effect upon the individual.

Problems.

To have stated the aim of education is already, in this case, to have pointed to certain difficulties. The first steps for achieving such an aim would be, it seems, to introduce into the school system new practices, followed regularly, for creating a contributive *habit.* If it is believed that there are certain basic instincts which, when allowed free play, find expression in contribution, these must be given opening. School exercises will be needed which provide this opening. There must be corporate work for the scholars to do, and corporate results, so that the pooling of effort may acquire reality.

In other words, the type of education needed is one which, recognising in the individual native powers, interests, anxieties, will use and direct these along such channels that in the end they become outward-turned and creative. One condition for such an achievement is, however, the ability to invent ways in which these powers may, actually during school practices, be exercised thus. And this demands not one, but a wide variety of schemes of work essentially corporate.

By its very nature, however, school education allows little scope within it for such work. Its fundamental activity is that of developing *in each individual* a certain competence. And from this type of activity there appears to be no escape.

Since there does not exist a corporate mind subject to education, nor any unit which is greater than or less than the individual mind, it follows that the task of mental training is to produce, not one corporate efficiency, but efficiency in each of the distinct units. Each is to be prepared separately as an instrument. Thus, by reason of the character of this educational task, there is little power to bring into it corporate forms of exercise, or of providing the means whereby individuals may, as a habit, contribute.

Such service aspect as education does in fact possess lies beyond the group in which the actual training is undertaken. At the end of the period of instruction each instrument is sent forth to serve, not the small body of associates with whom it has been trained, but the wider body of society into which all preparatory groups merge. Thus the object of the education, and the field in which it yields its contribution, are remote in time and place from the instruction. During the actual period of the training attention is inevitably focussed solely on the individual. Its effect is therefore to foster self-concern. And it impedes the growth of a more ample vision.

From these first difficulties various other problems arise. Since the aim is to create competence in the individual, there is no means of success except through individual mental strife. Activity in each separate mind is needed in order that the mind may grow, and each gains power more or less in ratio to its own effort. Only to a small extent can one developing mind aid the enlargement of another; indeed, the attempt to give help often only hinders, causing the dependent mind to become still more dependent.

This individual work is as a rule done most genuinely and effectively if it can be pursued in an atmosphere of apartness, a condition such that the student is assured of freedom from interruption and—a vital point —may make his own pace. For memory work, and for inventive or artistic work, it is peculiarly urgent that each should have a separate retreat.

Furthermore, from the point of view of strengthening some aspects of personality, independence of work is needed. Self-reliance and originality, which are indispensable as personal assets whether for business or for any other later career, can be formed only if all stand alone both in the acquisition and in the use of their knowledge.

Finally, the tests must be of the individual. Even were it desirable to find some means of testing groups, this could not be done; for, as seen, there is only one unit, the individual mind, to test. Although it is true that by totalling individual results a quasi-group-result may be shown, this is not in reality an index of group efficiency, but only an abstract computation from individual efficiencies. As such it has little meaning, and it is valueless for later, outside purposes, since the concern of those who take educated persons into their employ is to know the quality of each person separately. The method of totalling individual results may have, as will be shown, a certain value for encouraging the pooling of efforts towards a group achievement and for developing a common interest; but it can only supplement, and not supplant, the individual test.

Thus from the inherent character of education and from the demands made of it, there will be found the utmost difficulty in creating through its practices a contributive habit. To change these practices radically so that through them each person might add regularly to a group result would in many subjects mean loss of efficiency. In general it might have the effect of weakening independence, and of reducing in particular the competence of those who already lack resource.

It seems therefore that the furthest advance towards the aim held in view, that is, towards the develop-

ment of a system which will allow play to the service
motive, will be the adoption of methods representing
some compromise between, or combination of, individual and corporate work. The disadvantages of corporate work do not affect equally all branches of
study. Within the wide range of subjects in ·the
curriculum there will be found some, the corporate
treatment of which, whilst yielding partly the disadvantages shown here, may offset these through the
extra stimulus gained from the social character of the
work. Especially would a prospect of such gain seem ·
to arise in the sphere of history, drama, economics,
and the relatively straightforward parts of science
which lend themselves to joint experiment.

One of the first aims of a movement for the evolution of school method would thus be to scrutinise all
subjects taken, to distinguish clearly between those
branches in which individual work remains imperative,
and those in which corporate work may, without undue weakening of the system, be substituted.

The Need for Diversity of Method.

To devise a single, simple scheme of education
capable of producing widely any motive, or way of
thought, would seem by its nature an aim beyond
realisation. The crystallisation of methods into one
set scheme must of itself tend to defeat this aim; for,
a rigid system, however theoretically perfect, leads as
a rule to two main results, neither of which may be

I

said justly to imply the development of a free and fully alert motive. Its effect upon the more pliable, suggestible group of students is to cast them in the form of a mould, as stereotyped, scarcely inspired creatures of the system. The nonconformists, on the other hand, react against the system, escaping from it as the reverse of the customary mould.

There is a further reason for bewaring of undue systematisation. No system, it would seem, can have the least influence ethically, or towards the creation of motive, unless the staff applying it hold its philosophy. The system alone is useless, being dependent for its quickening upon those who make use of it as their instrument. Hence there can be little gain from evolving a careful, compact scheme of education for application to all conditions : rather the aim would be to discover the appropriate staff and aid them to the formation of their own system.

A relevant example of this inability to frame a special educational scheme to achieve an ethical aim arises from the problem, much discussed, of modifying the system to include or exclude religion. Surely the essence of the finding in this case must be that the nature of the system is of no significance whatever; it can make little difference whether the religion is formally included or not : for if the teacher has no religion he will convey nothing, except a little history, even though the subject be included ; if he has religion it will escape from him and have its effect with or with-

out the actual lesson.   The problem is primarily one
of staff selection, rather than of the composition of the
system.

The same may perhaps be said with yet greater
force where the aim is to create a motive.   A system
no matter how meticulously framed to give play to a
certain motive would fail to reach its aim and would
probably break down completely, if applied by those
who had not sensed its philosophy.   Indeed, in this
aspect of educational effort, it seems not too much to
say that the system *is* the teacher, and that when the
teacher goes the system must go also.   Sanderson
of Oundle evolved a unique scheme, and succeeded
brilliantly, but his withdrawal meant the gradual
recession of the scheme : and nowhere else, apparently,
has its revival been found possible.   Such instances
might be multiplied to show that a system, like
clothing, may fit one person well but not others, and
that it may be folly to attempt the devising of any
school system for use by all.   The more exceptional
the aim, the more exceptional will be the teacher who
can further it, and the fewer will be those who can
clothe themselves with the appropriate system for
attaining it.

The conclusion to which this must revert, then, and
the finding on which the rest of the chapter is based, is
that the aim of any movement for the development of
motive should be, not the preparation of a single,
concerted scheme of education, but the accumulation

of a series of varied " devices," exercises or practices, which may be applied widely in schools for setting alight the desired motive.   There would be a special gain, for instance, from the publication of a symposium of past experiments, or of possible or suggested experiments, through which instruction has been or may be without loss converted into a corporate activity.. From such a source of suggestion any teacher having the contributive philosophy and wishing to spread it might make a selection of methods suited to his special conditions, and test them in further practice. This, in turn, would imply additional experience which, if again collated, would enlarge the basis for expansion.

In the education of motive it is clear that the ideal to be held in view is the creation of an essentially dynamic habit : a habit which is adaptable to different spheres, times and conditions ; and a habit that is positive, implying the desire to seek, without external stimulus, the means to contribute.   Such an ideal is a far aim, given the most perfect methods ; but one first condition of its attainment is the power to vary methods.   For this reason it would seem that the experiments in mind here should cover a wide field of interests, all avenues for corporate work being explored both within the scope of school work proper and in the club, house, class, field and camping activities which go with it.

Effective illustration of the suggestion outlined is perhaps not realisable in a single chapter ; but the aim in the remaining pages will be as far as possible to show, by sample, the type of experiment which has been tried and found successful, and the type which would necessarily form the basis of any symposium of " devices " which might be made. Some reference will be made first to university method, then to developments in adolescent and early education.

The University.

Although it is mainly upon the lecture system that universities rely for instruction, this appears to be the result rather of tradition than of any conscious growth of educational theory. The lecture has without question certain technical merits not present in other methods, and is probably unequalled as a medium for didactic explanation or pure description. Further, it has one outstanding quality which will prevent its being supplanted readily, namely, that it can deal with numbers. It is a mass production method, and as such it is likely to outlive most competing methods.

Despite this strength it shows certain defects. As an aid to the assimilation of ideas it may deceive by its very offer of facility. Thought cannot be digested and absorbed until worked on by the receiving mind; thus unless the mind has opportunity to sift and scrutinise ideas as they arise, they will for the most part be let slip. Clearly the lecture leaves small opening for such contemplation, since to dwell on any particular thought in it is to lose its essential thread.

Moreover, a thought remains " inert," to use White-
head's term, until it has become vitalised by being
related to life and practice. And it is un-coordinated,
and worthless for a scheme of knowledge, until it has
been fitted into its place in wider science. Hence the
effect of a lecture may often be to spread half-seized,
" inert," and unschematised ideas, there being no
adequate time for thought-gestation in the few spaces
between notes.

Because the system is the acknowledged university
basis, it favours the impression that the task of self-
education is complete when the crumbs of thought
have been garnered from the lecture. It gives a certain hall-mark of approval to light thinking. For the
same reason it may induce the student to rely for information on the spoken rather than on the written
word, and he may in consequence form no easy acquaintance with the source of knowledge which is both
the widest at the university and virtually the only one
available later. He may lean unduly on the immediate pedagogue, thus failing to acquire that independence which is a first condition of strong development
later.

From the particular point of view of this chapter,
the lecture system can lend no aid. There is not a
hint of co-operation in it. The lecturer is out of real
touch with the listeners, and, in general, they contribute
no thought throughout the course.

Whatever may be its shortcomings, the system, as

noted, is due for long service.   There is apparently
no other ready means of handling numbers; and in
future the number of students per staff member may
increase, not because less funds are given for education but because they may be applied mainly to
introduce more students.   Thus the only reasonable
prospect seems to be that of compensating any undesired effects of the lecture system by the addition,
where possible, of other methods.   Such other
methods would initially be supplementary to, rather
than substitutes for, the lecture system; but in course
of time they might be extended to rank equally with it.

The most effective alternative, applied in universities now to a limited extent but capable of development, is the Seminar system.   This implies, when
fully matured, a method whereby from fifteen to
twenty persons combine in the study of some subject
which lends itself to discussion.   The subject is
divided and sub-divided into a course of themes, related and consecutive, each theme being capable of
treatment briefly in, say, a twenty minutes' paper.
These are then distributed among the group so that
each has his share to prepare.   When a meeting is held,
the member whose theme is due to be examined reads
his paper; and discussion follows.   The instructor's
task is to chart the course, provocatively; to give
references and aid the members' research; and to
ensure that the discussion converges on some fairly
concise result.

The gains from the method are perhaps more potential than assured. Its chief merit, socially, is that each member escapes the unhappy rôle of mere mental sponge and becomes himself a contributor. And since giving out is fundamentally of more interest than taking in, activity tends to be sustained. Further, relations change. Instead of one voice incessantly, twenty may be at work; and the relations which develop become scarcely conscious, therefore perfect for the exchange of thought and attitude.

The method is one which lends itself equally to poor results. In group discussion, as in boxing, a high skill may emerge or mere brawling : a certain poise and restraint, or offensiveness. But the atmosphere is such that high quality results may, with fair management, ensue.

From a purely technical point of view the Seminar method shows a certain definite superiority. It increases mental speed; ideas raised in discussion are contemplated actively forthwith, and become related and no longer " inert "; the members are obliged to acquire a certain independence, and a mastery at least in one sphere sufficient to lead others; and a wide acquaintance is made with books.

These advantages are at present offset by the fact that the system involves a ratio of one staff member per subject to twenty students, whereas the lecture system can change the ratio to one in eighty, a hundred, or more.

An experiment which might however be attempted with a view to accommodating the Seminar system to larger numbers would be as follows : The members of the group, having received the series of themes, would work thereafter independently of the instructor, as a committee, formed with speaker and reporter appointed in rotation, and would report on each theme within a time limit. To give a directive to discussions a *questionnaire*, setting out specific points on which the report should range, would be issued by the instructor. He might, in addition, appear at strategic intervals to give special aid; but apart from this his guidance would be given through comment on reports submitted, and perhaps through occasional specimen " ideal " reports.

Such a method would be applicable, if desired, to extramural students. It would become then the equivalent of a correspondence course, with the distinction that answers would be submitted, not by individuals separately, but by a Seminar or group.

Adolescent and Early Education.[1]

" Let all schools be closed at once," cried D. H. Lawrence. " The ideal mind, the brain, has become the vampire of modern life, sucking up the blood and the life. There is hardly an original thought or original

[1] Much of the remainder of this chapter has been written by M. E. Frances Bellerby, whose practical work as teacher gives a discrimination not possible to the present writer.

utterance possible to us. All is sickly repetition of stale, stale ideas . . . Let all schools be closed at once. Keep only a few technical training establishments, nothing more. Let humanity lie fallow, for two generations at least. Let no child learn to read, unless it learns by itself, out of its own individual persistent desire . . . Education means leading out the individual nature in each man and woman to its true fullness. You can't do that by stimulating the mind. To pump education into the mind is fatal. That which sublimates from the dynamic consciousness into the mental consciousness has alone any value."

" My education," Bernard Shaw has remarked, " was somewhat hindered by my schooling."

Schooling that was a millstone about a child's neck was not a feature of the nineteenth century only. It has remained in more than shadow; and this is not because the " old " notions are preferred now by those who teach, but because they form one scheme of which all parts cohere. Being concerted, in its way the old system works. And it will continue to work and yield at least some intellectual result so long as no incoherent element be mingled with it. It was founded on belief in fear and the competitive instinct, and, with true logic, pressed on to its results with the aid of force, authority, penalties and prizes, tradition and conventional rule. Whilst no variation from such methods is made the system may be relied upon to make possible

the attainment of definitely known standards.   There
is safety in it.   But if new half-measures are introduced, so that the appeal is made, now to fear and the
competitive instinct, now to interest and the co-operative will, disaster follows.   A hybrid system inevitably
fails.   The new ideas, tested in an atmosphere which
is foreign to them or unprepared, are rejected, being
thrown aside because they can make no adequate
blend with the prevailing scheme.

" Belief in the child " may be said to be the central
point from which the experiments of to-day radiate.
There is now a changed emphasis, so that no longer is
the chief aim felt to be to *impose* knowledge upon the
child from without, but rather to seek his own interests and keep them fresh.   If his mind may be kept
always alert *from within*, learning must follow.   " Not
knowledge or information, but self-realisation, is the
goal . . .   Moreover, subject-matter never can be
got into the child from without.   Learning is active.
It involves reaching out of the mind.   It involves
organic assimilation starting from within.   Literally,
we must take our stand with the child and our departure from him.   It is he and not the subject-
matter which determines both quality and quantity
of learning." [1]   This, says John Dewey, is the opinion
of the sect whose watchword is " Interest," as opposed
to " Discipline " of another sect.

First, then, according to the new system, must be

[1] John Dewey, *The Child and the Curriculum.*

discovered the instincts which are latent in every child. These found, he must be led to use, to develop them, and thereby develop himself. Nothing in him need be thwarted. All energies may be tempered, disciplined, guided; but they must be given scope. For it is believed that through them in time will grow that integrated being of body, mind and spirit which is a " well-educated man."

Since it seems that there can exist within a child no impulse that has not its origin in some purpose, the teacher's work is to find the purpose, in each case, and make its attainment possible. This is another way of saying : discover what are the child's own interests; then find the purpose of these interests; then lay a train directly from the interests to the purpose. This, it would seem, is the logic which underlies Play as the earliest path to learning. Most modern experimenters would hold, with Froebel, that " Play at first is just natural life," and with R. L. S. that " Happy play in grassy places " has always been the essential means by which " children grew to kings and sages." John Dewey says of Play that it is " not to be identified with anything which the child externally does. It rather designates his mental attitude in its entirety and in its unity. It is the free play, the interplay, of all the child's powers, thoughts, and physical movements, in embodying, in a satisfying form, his own images and interests."

The Playway, by Caldwell Cook, is probably the

best-known description of experimenting on these lines. It is a delightful account of the work-play of the author and his " Littlemen " (boys up to thirteen), in whose hands the precept " That we would do we should do when we would " is not a dangerous, but a wise and life-giving one.

Mr. Cook's personality imbues each page, as it must have done each step of the Playway. Indeed an obvious thought is that nobody but a Caldwell Cook could make a success with these methods, and his kind does not abound. It is true that in the hands of a mediocre teacher, someone lacking sympathy, tact, personality, a sense of humour, this way would probably be the shortest road to futility. But this is not necessarily a criticism of the system.

The foremost aim of this appeal to the child's own interests is to make and keep education *alive*, and in this the Playway was undoubtedly successful. There was no " inert knowledge " among the Littlemen. There was furiously eager life. They played tirelessly : they dramatised, produced, acted, and mimed; they made a miniature Playtown, out-of-doors, complete with such details as harbour, railway, bridges, and—eventually—a local paper; they drew up plans of imaginary " ilonds," and wrote poems describing them, which were put into chap-books; they followed a custom of giving short original lectures, at which a " Hammer-boy " (whose name denotes his occupation) officiated; they had a " Knightly Guard " consisting of a Knight-Captain and six others, knighted for "deeds of prowess or renown," whose responsibility it was to give out homework, see that desks were in order, and the like; they were accustomed to a pin-drop as the dismissal-signal from class.

Such were some of the Playway details. It will readily be seen that they were of a kind to make the co-operative spirit leap. In the depths of this book there dwells a sense of that live unity, spreading from the high inventor, which gathers to it all co-inventors and co-seekers after life.

Edmond Holmes's Utopian school, described in *What is and What Might Be*, is inspired by the same certainty that the whole business of education must make its start from within the child. " In Utopia the school life of the children is all play—play taken very seriously, play systematised, organised, provided with ample materials and ample opportunities, encouraged and stimulated in every possible way. Each of the fundamental instincts that manifest themselves in the child's play . . . is duly administered to in this school . . . " The author then names these fundamental instincts, describing in some detail the Utopian methods of developing each one.

For the sake of the communicative instinct, children and school-mistress (" Egeria ") hold " free conversation," the first thing each morning. Then the children tell Egeria about anything that has caught their interest—that they may have seen,

heard, imagined, thought—anything whatever cross-
ing their inner or outer paths. Egeria listens, sym-
pathises, encourages, responds (she is a rarely delightful person, but there is not the least reason to suppose
that she must be non-existent).

The ingenious treatment of the dramatic and the
artistic instincts in this school need not be dwelt
upon here, since actual schools to be mentioned later
give convincing illustration of the same treatment.
And similarly, the inquisitive and constructive instincts, which receive unceasing ministrations in this
Utopia, are recognised in existing schools. What
should be said here is that Edmond Holmes has shown
a theory, complete, and has revealed it in motion.
The theory is such that all thoughts on education may
with safety be linked to it. The instincts which he
mentions exist; we may wish to give them different
labels; or we may wish to rank them differently;
but they exist. It is the experience of all who have
worked with children that, in each one, there is the
impulse to communicate, in the shy and uncommuni-
cative perhaps most strongly of all; to act and dramatise; to seek, and express, beauty; to find out things;
and to make things. If these impulses are named
Communicative, Dramatic, Artistic, Inquisitive and
Constructive, this is only to call them by their known
everyday expression. Not only do these exist, but—
the thought of chief weight here—they end, each one,
in creativeness. Hence the aim of education should

be to fan these sparks into flame, so that in full time
they may yield that high contributiveness which
comes from anxiety to build, and exhilaration in building, the things of fair presence and fair idea. Thus,
Edmond Holmes concludes : " When the growth of
the soul is healthy and harmonious, the cultivation of
all the expansive instincts having been fully provided
for, the *communal* instinct will evolve itself in its
own season ; and when the communal instinct has been
fully evolved, the social order will begin to reform
itself."

J. Howard Whitehouse has written *Creative Education at an English School*, describing Bembridge, where
the development of the creative instincts is definitely
the chief aim of the curriculum. The book is illustrated partly by examples of the boys' work in woodcutting, water-colours, carpentry, and pottery; the
evident imaginative power, æsthetic sense, and crafts-
manship, are impressive. If there are still those who
affirm that boys and girls, except the gifted few,
can only " muddle around " at such things, wasting
everybody's time and much money, the quality of the
work done at Bembridge by all the boys as regular
school subjects should certainly leave them silent.

Some notable features are : the inclusion in the
time-table of Woodcutting and Carpentry, and Garden-
ing for all forms below the Upper Fourth. The possession of a printing-press (a school-paper, brought out
each term, is produced entirely by the boys; written,

printed, and bound in covers engraved with original designs). Work at Pottery, out of regular school-hours. The existence, independently of class-teaching, of a Scientific, and an Art Society, holding meetings at which original papers are read; and of a Sketching Club which gives Sunday morning exhibitions. The custom by which groups of boys make books illustrating well-known poems or tales—different boys, or several boys together, being responsible for different parts. An occasional co-operative experiment such as that entirely voluntary one which resulted in the publication of " Bembridge, an Historical and General Survey "; or an illustrated book which one form produced, called " A Form Room Fellowship." The termly production of a school-play obviously managed without the extinction of most of the time-table which so often accompanies this feat. The holding of three annual school exhibitions : a general school exhibition in summer; and in the spring and autumn a display related to some definite subject such as " National Arts and Crafts," " Model Engineering," " American Architecture."

Through these varied pursuits great breadth of expression is made possible to the five leading instincts from which, following Edmond Holmes, we may expect the growth finally of the communal instinct. The Artistic and the Dramatic are restlessly at work. The Inquisitive and the Constructive join forces unceasingly. Whilst these impulses give the drive

K

needed to maintain high activity, the activity itself is corporate. The play is throughout that of the whole group. In time it will be the combined expression not of the existing community merely, but of a continuous emergent being.

It is a far cry from Bembridge to the Caldecott Community, but both schools have that fundamental notion of developing what Mr. Whitehouse calls " noble interests in Life," and both set out to do this by means of creative work—by appeal to the primitive expansive instincts. The Community, founded as a nursery school some twenty years ago, is now a boarding school near Cheshunt, in Hertfordshire, where working-men's children—chiefly " normal children from abnormal homes "—are educated. Staff and children co-operate over the tasks of the community life, living simply and working much, since there is no money in the background. Perception of beauty, and the expression of this in terms of self-realisation, is an aim which seems to pervade the curriculum; and the extent of the success may be estimated by the quality of entertainment provided at the annual dramatic performance given in London by the Community. Here is evident not only wit, skill and grace; but also, reflected in young, sensitive, imaginative sympathies, and intense appreciation, that rare disconcerting presence, Beauty.

In this school the Montessori system is used for the juniors, Dalton for the seniors. The Dalton plan, emphatically one of learning, not of being taught, is

probably more in line than any other with the trend
of modern ventures; indeed, many are adaptations
from it. In essence, its purpose is to extend those
conditions of freedom and personal initiative, which
exist now for the doing of " home-work," to work
done on school premises, so that even here the scholar
is master of his own times and movements. The
work is assigned in groups of tasks, the whole armoury
of modern educational inventions being used to make
these tasks appeal to interest. Then, the point of
chief significance, not only are personal exchanges
and mutual aid permitted during hours, they
are encouraged. Each becomes a member of a
free society, independent if he wishes, social if he
wishes.[1]

At Kingsmoor, in Derbyshire, the Dalton system is
in use for children of eleven and onwards. The distinctive feature of the system as applied here is that
with its aid, it is claimed, it has been possible to
eliminate competition almost entirely, and to do
away altogether with prizes and punishments. This
accomplishment is strengthened by the further unusual
practice of including philosophy in the curriculum as
a regular school subject. The teaching is based on
the words and lives of great men of all races and times,
including, with especial emphasis, the ethical principles of Christ as providing " the only clear way of
life consistent with progress." [2]

[1] See *Education on the Dalton Plan*, by Helen Parkhurst.
[2] *The New Era*, July, 1928.

The " Recapitulatory Theory " has now many adherents, and two outstanding movements, the Order of Woodcraft Chivalry and the Kibbo Kift, base their educational policy upon it. Believing that every man repeats, in the course of his development, the stages of development through which the whole race has passed, they hold that modern civilisation is an environment totally unsuited to a child; for it is the farthest stage from that which by primitive instinct he is recapitulating. He ought to be learning in the way that all other young animals learn—from Nature. This is where every impulse towards self-assertiveness, domination, trial of strength, may be allowed full rein, being sublimated instead of thwarted. The most valuable of all individual powers, which when perverted lead to destructiveness, may be encouraged to expand in Nature's robust company. Thus whereas in the back streets of our slum-soiled cities there may generally be seen, about dusk, numbers of young human animals, playing their curiously thrilling games; tracking in gangs; rushing round corners; lurking in dark places; dodging policemen; flashing lights in half-built, echoing houses; tunnelling holes in some scrap of waste land, to spend long dark evenings there, with candles, books, cigarettes, food—guarded from Authority by a look-out boy—the romantic, self-assertive instincts which drive them there might be used, if expressed with Nature, for creating lawful, but up-leaping personality.

These instincts are acclaimed by the Order and the Kindred as an essential part of Nature's educational equipment; and the immense value of camp life as a means of making use of them is emphasised vigorously by both movements. The Kibbo Kift wish to see every town school with its camp counterpart; the Order of Woodcraft Chivalry suggests that rural schools should be " housed " in a camp consisting of " congeries of small tents, clustered together, but not necessarily in any exact order, and placed upon some wild but sheltered piece of ground not more than half-an-hour's walk from the town or village where the children live. One or two larger tents, or a wooden hut, should be provided for common purposes, as for cooking, dining, or for a resort in bad weather—and such shelters might be suitably provided by the Education Authority . . . The camp would serve also for small parties of city children, and would form a centre for all sorts of scout, woodcraft, and natural history activities." The Order also advocates Travelling School-Camps, by which geography and history could be learnt more realistically than from books.

The founder of the Order, Ernest Westlake, originated and developed the idea of " Forest Schools," which would provide an environment suited to the child's needs. " The life itself," he said, would be the " means of instruction, just as it was in the past." He died before his hope could be realised, but not before he had chosen and acquired a site on the western edge of the New Forest, overlooking the Avon valley. Here, in 1929, " The Forest School " was founded. It is as yet a very small community, but it is an actual beginning, a first expression of a " deep desiring thought." Here staff and children live co-operatively, sharing household tasks, and the children use the primitive arts as ways of " learning by doing." The proximate aim in Ernest Westlake's Forest School conception, was that by general experience and training each child should be fitted for any later specialisation; the ultimate aim, that as many instincts and potentialities as possible should be encouraged to develop in each child, excepting only such as would clash with his social environment; at the existing school the fullest possible self-expression is regarded as " the most rational road to learning."

The educational beliefs of the Kibbo Kift Kindred would appear to be in their *practical* results similar to those of the Order; *theoretically*, they differ, because the general policies, other than educational, of the two movements, are avowedly different. There is at Caldbeck, in Cumberland, a three-year-old co-educational school, Friar Row, which although it is not labelled Kibbo Kift seems to be founded and run upon ideas which are in sympathy with the Kindred's; and its head-mistress is a Kinswoman. The value of experience, especially that gained from wild nature, is the basic belief; and the site was chosen for its

educational possibilities; by the strong aid of river,
hills, sea, and an atmosphere vivid with history and
tradition, the children are to be " educated for Life."
They use their environment in many ways; by ex-
cursions, for instance, and occasional week-end camps,
and an outdoor life aiming at "the development
of a spirit of hardihood." Their activities, including
household tasks, are chiefly co-operative, the purpose
being to create "the atmosphere of a good home."

The descriptions in this brief outline of school
experiments have been given as separate, somewhat
disjointed fragments; they nevertheless blend into a
fairly compact theme. The purport of it is that there
exists, within the raw material, the essence of everything that can develop. In the acorn *is* the matured
oak-tree, in the potter's shapeless clay *is* a vase of
great beauty, in the slow, clumsy, unprepossessing
grub *is* the flashing, radiant, unbelievable dragon-fly.
And in the child is a Higher Thing than the most
visionary, optimistic, ambitious and inspired teacher
can describe; yet he may at least know that all the
raw material he needs is ready, there, to his hand.
All the growth that can take place in the child and
man will spring from the existing innate forces,
anxieties, interests. It remains only to encourage.
Play, therefore, is the ideal way in the beginning,
because it not only reveals these interests, but also,
by keeping them alert, promotes their growth.

Experiments such as those described in *The Playway* show this clearly.

It has been said that animals do not play because they are young, but they are given their youth because they must play. With young human life the purposiveness of play is disclosed in a later phase. Fortified by the emerging instincts to communicate, dramatise, design, seek out and build, play reveals itself as a most potent educational force; for from these inherent unconscious eagernesses grow creative strength, and a conscious, urgent, restlessness for expression. That a high result may be hoped for from this awakening is made evident by work achieved, notably at Bembridge.

The creativeness which is the end appointed for each of the play instincts need not stop short with the individual, but may spread through a group—a result that follows readily in schools where the work is corporate. Creativeness, with this aid, becomes contributiveness. The communal instinct, emerging, and having free expression, both gains and gives strength.

But at this stage there are those who would urge caution. Communal and spiritual development are not often realised early in life. Some children may be contributive almost from birth; but they are probably not of the majority. Accepting the young human animal as he is, not as we would like him to be, we realise that in immaturity there are restless forces that

are far from contributive in their first expression.
Let Nature deal with these. Let them go free, but in
the woods where they may break safely. Blind and
freakish though they may be, they should not be
stifled; for they are the drive behind all ultimate
poised constructiveness.

It has been seen that many schools are working now
with methods which in their full season may yield
this constructiveness. Many individuals now seem to
think the same kind of thoughts on education; some
speak and write them, some work them out in actual
experiments. But despite this significant convergence
of modern ideas, the theories, methods and experiments
would themselves seem of small account compared
with the will and attitude of those whose craft it is
to practise them. " Start with the child," is a good
slogan, but it would be as pertinent to urge "Start with
those who show the path." It is surely a terrifyingly
high vocation to have heard, even as a whisper,

> " . . . the voice that cries,
> ' Make the way smooth
> For the feet of the lord of the world,
> Whose name is youth.' "

CHAPTER VI

A CONTRIBUTIVE SOCIETY

THERE remains a considerable task. The first part of it is to define a motive, or a balance of motives, which, if it became general, might be expected to reinvigorate the economic system and remove those of its features which at present cause weakness. The second part of the task is to show that the motive-balance, as defined, would in fact give the desired new life and quality to the system.

The first problem, that of definition, is the easier of the two, and may be accomplished in a few paragraphs. The motive to be assumed here throughout as the basis of the economic system is that of " maximum contribution." This expression is necessarily used to suggest an impulse which is uppermost rather than in sole sway over conduct; for contribution itself implies acquisition. The urge to give is derived in part from the appreciation of the value of the things given : an appreciation which is possible only to those who themselves experience the wish to have. Thus intense contributiveness involves inevitably a strong power of enjoyment and a love of things. It gains strength from these, and adds only the anxiety to see them spread.

"Maximum contribution" may be defined as the will to add one's utmost to the community's total acquisition of goods and services and favours. It implies, on the one hand, that a person becomes a voluntary sweated labourer; and, on the other, that in consumption he applies the principle of averaging or sharing. Since it is to the community as a whole that the gift is to be made, the contributor necessarily ranks himself equally with all others for benefits; and he attempts to assess his share by making some estimate of the "average wage."

The attempt to limit consumption to this average, whilst following naturally upon any contributive urge, might nevertheless in some cases, by its reaction on the individual, reduce his power to serve; and in such cases "maximum contribution" would involve consumption greater than the average. The problem which this raises will have to be examined more fully shortly, but it may be assumed for the moment that, for most persons, the limitation of their expenditure to the average would increase the surplus which they could pool for the benefit of the group. If this is so, it may be said that, apart from exceptional cases, the principle of "maximum contribution" involves for the individual two things : first, maximum production; secondly, average consumption. The task which remains is to examine the efficiency of this principle as the basis of society.

This further problem of showing that the motive, as

described, would, if universalised, yield the results desired in the economic system, will involve a long analysis occupying much of the rest of the chapter. For the purpose of such an inquiry one assumption, and one only, will be permissible : that there exists a group of persons increasing progressively in numbers as time advances, who have the urge to make their " maximum contribution." The economic system which would emerge, on this assumption, will be shown as a series of stages of growth, being traced forward as the expansion of a society recruited from persons having the aim described.

The first stage in the discussion will thus be to consider the problems confronting a small experimental group in the immediate present. As an initial nucleus, their aim would be, by trial and adjustment, to establish such rules of economic conduct as would be mutually consistent and would conform to their basic contributive principle. They would have to adjust their business methods, personal expenditure, and treatment of property to produce a pattern which would be coherent as a system in the present and capable of preparing the way for a more distant future. And they would need to set up organisation in order to be of mutual assistance to one another in the application of the principles. These early problems of practical action by a group of prospectors will be considered first.

At a second stage in the account it will be necessary

to consider how far the principles and organisation set up by the early group would, in fact, be capable of extension, and what developments would be needed to accommodate large numbers. For this purpose a further conjectural situation must be shown, when the greater development of the Society will be assumed to have taken place. Possibly the situation to be forecast will lack the sense of reality in some respects; but the necessity cannot be escaped of showing that, as far as may be judged from any present vision, the organisation initially adopted would not be destined to break down merely through the increase of numbers.

At a final stage some reflection will be necessary upon the ultimate situation which would emerge if the principles were to become universal. Proof will be needed that the Society's rules could be extended to form the central features of an all-comprising economic system. Moreover—the point of real weight here—it should be possible to show that a system founded in this way, through the generalising of the contributive motive, would reach as high a rank as can reasonably be foreseen.

This three-stage account may now be taken up from the beginning. It may be given as a description of growth, in which the first stages are undoubtedly the most important.

THE INITIAL ORGANISATION OF THE SOCIETY.

It may be assumed that any urge to contribute effectively would drive those on whom it settled to the adoption of some form of organisation. Especially in the case of men who had an aim in common, and a mutual liking, would some definite association seem inevitable. Hence the beginning may be made here with the assumption that an organisation of one kind or another would emerge.

In coming together, any group would have to decide, as a first point, what should be their Society's requirement for admission. They would need to consider what was the essential common basis of their association, so that this might find reflection in the conditions of membership. In the present case, however, the one mutual bond and the one basic requirement would have been settled in advance. The condition from which the beginning is made is that each member shall be bent on making " maximum contribution."

Since this is the only requirement, the members would be concerned to know what exact meaning they should give to it. Certain difficulties would at once arise in the task of translating the aim into a common rule; although each individual might know what it signified for himself, there would be required in addition some definition to apply to all members —a definition which might be applied as a test of the sincerity of every individual's aim—and the discovery of this would not be easy.

One of the main difficulties arising in any such attempt to interpret "maximum contribution" is to decide whether, for the purpose of a Society, it should imply *invariably* the adoption of the "average wage" principle. The suggestion was made earlier that, in the majority of cases, "maximum contribution" would lead directly to the assumption of the average wage. Since the aim of the contributor under this rule is to enlarge his gift to the whole of society, all members of it being regarded as equal, he gives to himself, as one of society, at the most not more than his share. In other words, he confines his personal expenditure to the "average wage."

The fact that there are exceptions to the rule is, however, the source of chief difficulty. There are some persons who, by spending more than the average upon themselves, succeed in giving still more to society; and when they do this, both they and society benefit. In these cases the principle of "maximum contribution" does not lead to the average wage, but conflicts with it. What, then, is the Contributive Society to do? Is it to exclude those who cannot conform to the "average wage," or is it to include them on the understanding that they are bent on maximum contribution?

The cases may not be relatively numerous; but they seem to be most important. In the production of the most sensitive artistic work it frequently happens that efficiency depends upon conditions entirely psychic: freedom from intrusion, change of scene, the sea and the mountains, gaiety—all of which may involve outlay much in excess of that which is possible to every man. Then there are those who have the talent and energy to spend ten or twelve hours of the day contributing at a high level of efficiency to others, and preferring to do this rather than attend to their own needs. But if they have no time to look after themselves, they will want more help from others, and may, perhaps, be compelled to consume more than the average of the services of others.

For an individual so placed the sensible thing to do, presumably, would be to continue exceeding the average consumption. Since the effect of an increase in his consumption is to help him to create a still greater increase in his production, and since in this there is advantage to all, there can be little virtue in his doing otherwise than consume whatever excess is needed.

Whether, however, the newly forming Society would be well advised to include in its membership all such contributors, irrespective of their inability to limit themselves to the average wage, seems less certain. There are other reasons, mainly of expediency, which would make the average wage principle peculiarly attractive as a practical rule for the Society. It has, in the first place, the supreme virtue of clear expression, and of interpretation in terms of money. It is something tangible and fairly definite. It draws a line which all can see, and seeing, realise whether they are or are not conforming. Moreover, once this line is deserted, there is no landmark left whatever.

As a backbone to the Society's rules, the " average wage " principle might thus be peculiarly helpful; and in all probability it would be preserved as the main practical guide—the guide to be followed at least by the majority of the members.

There are nevertheless some considerable risks inherent in rules of this nature, by reason either of their being too rigid, or of their emphasising the letter and not the spirit of the principle. Thus, when it is urged that rigidity is especially helpful, and that a firm principle, like the weak man's armour, serves to protect him when he is off guard, it may be replied that such rigid armour may at times become a strait-jacket. Its effect is to restrict movement or expansion from within. Thus, in the case of the average wage, although this rule may be greatly strengthening in a man's protective code, it may often be a serious restraint, because of its rigidity, on his full power of expression.

Perhaps the more serious danger in such a rule is that it drives attention away from the spirit of observance to the external form. If the Society's approved test of motive is mere willingness to conform to the " average wage," the members will at all times

L

tend to rest content if they comply with this superficial money test.   They may forget that what is of essential point is whether their underlying motive remains unweakened.   In essence, the only kind of test by which a person can discover the inner reality of his aims is whether he chafes perpetually and increasingly at the city's sordidness; whether the sight of shoddy hurts him; whether he grudges everything stupidly spent; and whether he knows himself for poor quality when, for fear of appearing strange he continues to spend stupidly.   These are not necessarily the actual tests, but they show the kind of test which alone would seem capable of telling a person what his motives are.   To substitute any other kind, such as the acceptance of the " average wage," is dangerous, in that it diverts emphasis away from the essential towards the superficial.

Again, the " average wage " principle is sometimes commended because whoever complies with it conforms to the greater principle of equality.   Since equality is regarded as, in itself, an ideal, the " average wage " rule, being the practical expression of equality, is held similarly to be ideal.   But here, once again, there appears to be a risk of directing attention on the external thing, rather than on that which is beneath. Indeed, largely owing to this false emphasis, much of the current discussion on equality is entirely void. The real concern is to know, not whether equality is good, but whether there is good in fellow-feeling, imagination and other sympathies. If these existed, equality, or something like it, would just happen. If generosity were found everywhere, the problem of the present time would be, not whether equality and the average wage are good, but how to prevent the enthusiasm for give and take from flattening out the whole world into equality and uniformity. The difficulty would be how, in the general movement towards equality, it might be possible to make men put more enlightenment into giving and preserve to some extent variety and communal beauty.

The conclusions which may be drawn as regards the practical rule which the members of the Society might follow would thus seem to be somewhat diverse. Recognising that men are subject to fluctuations of strength and motives, the majority of the members would probably be disposed to adopt for their personal guidance the principle of the " average wage," this being the only rule which gives a definite entrench-ment in times of doubt. Moreover, they would probably wish to ensure that the number of excep-tions to this rule within the membership of the Society should be small, and might adopt some provision limiting the number. But, in order to preserve a due scepticism as to the virtues of the external rule and the external form, they would almost certainly not only allow a few exceptions to the average wage rule within their membership, but also recognise as a matter of independent merit any way of life which brought expenditure materially below the average.

For greater clarity in what ensues, it may be convenient to assume that members of the Society would in general be living at a level of expenditure about equal to the " average wage." The discussion may for the most part be continued concretely in terms of the " average wage," as if this were the practical rule adopted by the Society more or less as a whole. But if this device is used for simplicity and clearness, it should not mask the fact that the " average wage " is here held to be subsidiary to the contributive idea, and is at the best only a practical aid to anyone for whom it means no undue restriction of service.

One further note should be added, perhaps, to make clear what is the assumed basis from which the reasoning starts. If the principle of the average wage were to be adopted by most members of the Contributive Society, some variation in the limits of consumption fixed would be necessary according to the responsibilities of the members concerned. Just as, in present conditions, the average income for whole families is some 30 per cent. above the average wage for a single adult, a family in the Contributive Society would live at a higher level than a bachelor or spinster. Thus, the weekly figures fixed might be, say, 60s. for a single adult, 80s. for a married couple one of whom remained at home, and an additional 10s. for each dependent child. Whatever the difference might be, however, between one category and another, the aim would be to ensure that if all members of the employee community, including salaried persons, were to be paid according to the scale adopted, the amount received would be approximately equal to the total wages and salaries bill now being paid.

From this stage onwards, when references are made to the average wage, the term will be used with the above qualifications in mind.

The Purposes of the Society.

Men can be effectively united as a society only by their desire to pursue some mutual aim. Whenever there exists an aim, such as the ascent of Mount Everest, or the winning of a campaign, appropriate organisation forms itself, as it were, around the aim; and men are bound together, through the medium of the organisation, by reason of their interest in the aim.

Thus if the Contributive Society is to be dynamic and have a sound and deliberate organisation, it must possess at the outset a clear statement of its objects. Anxiety to contribute is not by itself sufficient; the members must know precisely towards what ends they would contribute. And before they can organise or associate they must be agreed on identical ends.

Viewed in a practical light, the question resolves itself into that of determining upon what objects the members might spend their surplus earnings. If each member succeeds in cutting personal expenditure to about the average wage, a considerable surplus of income must remain for other uses; and the problem at once arises : What uses are to be chosen ?

The task of reaching agreement on this point might not be simple. When it is remembered that the aims selected would represent the focus, not merely of spare-time or casual interest, but of the entire business and social enterprise of the members, it is clear that they would need to strike deep. They would have to be based on something of the nature of an agreed life-philosophy. Indeed, the immediate task confronting members would seem to be to settle their views as to the purpose of this whole earthly scheme; for only then could they derive a reasoned judgment as to the activities worthy to command their substance.

In a publication to be issued later[1] some discussion is to be attempted of the question of " Fundamental Values "—that is, purposes which seem to justify to the full economic and other effort. The necessity for a similar discussion by the prospective members of the Contributive Society is evident. They would need to determine at the outset what they wished to achieve for the individual and for the community. They would have to answer the question : What do we desire *for man* ?

[1] Probable title : *The Conflict of Values.*

A Statement of Common Aims.

Assuming that some measure of agreement might be reached on this question, the description of the Society's aims might be given in a two-fold form, partly philosophical, partly practical. There might be made, first of all, a statement of the wider ideals conceived by the Society as embracing all its aims : the increase of knowledge; the spread of art and beauty; the befriending of persons in need; the widening of fellowship. Such broader aims might then be expressed anew in the form of current, practical works, and a more definite outline given of the projects, industrial and social, which would be undertaken by the Society in pressing forward its aims.

Thus there might be a conscious acceptance by the Society of the abstract ideal of " spreading knowledge " and a practical attempt to reach out towards this ideal through, say : experiment in educational method; the setting up of schools; the endowment of libraries, art schools, research institutions, museums; adult education and the formation of evening classes; the publication of social literature; the provision of scholarships.

If " the spread of art and beauty " were an accepted aim, the beginning would necessarily be made by an attack on unsightliness. The practical aims might be : the clearing of slums; the protection of open spaces; the abolition of factors of dirt, smoke, noise, disease; the preservation of rural beauty; the provision of facilities for travel; the endowment of opera, sculpture, architecture, and exhibitions of new art.

Under " welfare and fellowship " there would be unlimited scope : the provision of boys' and girls' clubs and playgrounds; the organising of holiday camps; the reform of prisons, penitentiaries, workhouses, asylums; the work of hospital almoner; the care of old persons and of children with unsatisfactory homes; the giving of legal advice to the poor; industrial welfare work; the promotion of goodwill in industry; the promotion of international peace.

It may be expected that the Society would strive to supplement rather than to overlap the services ordinarily provided by the state or city. Similarly it would tend to give less support to works already commanding a steady flow of private subscriptions, such as universities, memorials, or publications, in order to concentrate upon the gaps in social activity. Thus in the case of education, since provision is already made for all persons to get some degree of education, the chief aim of the Society would be to experiment in methods. Its only way of adding substantially to what exists would be to discover new and more efficient ways of teaching, and systems which will yield better human material. Again, in the attempt to preserve or contrive things of beauty, the Society would concern itself less with public art galleries, municipal parks, and national monuments, than with the protection of fragments of beauty and countryside places that ordinarily escape official care.

All works such as the above, listed as suitable for inclusion in the statement of purposes of the Society, might for convenience be briefly described as its " common purposes." This term will be used here throughout to include every practical activity of a social nature upon which the members of the Society are agreed.

In addition to these " common purposes," each member would presumably have as many individual aims as he wished. Religion and local charities would seem to be most suitably considered as matters for the individual's private concern; and political affairs could not well fall within the scope of the Society considered as an entity.

Business Conduct.

Assuming that all members of the Society had found agreement sufficiently upon their aims, their next concern would be to seek the various means of promoting them. One method would be directly through work in industry. If any member were an architect, or a teacher, or a welfare worker, or a manufacturer of artistic wares, he would be contributing directly to the stated aims of the Society. Another method would be through deriving funds from work in industry and devoting them to the " common purposes."

Whatever method were adopted, the Society would

be concerned to ensure that its activity in business was such as to promote, either directly or through the supply of funds, its accepted objects. And to this end it would scrutinise carefully all methods, processes, or business " habits " to determine which, in fact, conformed to its tests.

As regards the actual industrial occupations to be followed, little more might perhaps be necessary than to exclude those which were definitely non-constructive or superfluous. These would be very few indeed. If any branches whatever of industry, or any professions, serve a direct purpose in the enhancement of life, then all the remaining sections of industry on which these branches or professions depend are serving indirectly the same purpose. Virtually it may be said that, either the whole of industry is non-constructive, or the whole of it is constructive. There are, indeed, certain activities which are parasitic, and others which the Society might regard as detrimental : some forms of speculation ; unnecessary commercial operations ; the provision of conveniences for gambling ; the manufacture of certain drugs and spirits ; and the publication of obscene literature. Some of these occupations would necessarily be banned ; but, in drawing up the rules the Society might perhaps confine itself to a general statement that all branches of industry which were not in conflict with its wider aims might be taken up by members.

As regards the methods, or business " habits," to be

adopted in industry and professions, the problems arising would be very much more complex. The members of the Society would find themselves working, either as employers or as employees, in an economic régime in which certain methods were already established; and these might or might not accord with the aims of the Society. For instance, it may be said of the " habit of competition," a firmly grounded business custom, that in certain cases it is wasteful, that in other cases it renders straight dealing impossible, and that, in consequence, it satisfies neither the Society's test of " maximum contribution," nor its possible desire to promote goodwill in industry. This " habit " therefore calls for investigation, to determine how far it can be accepted as falling within the approved code. Many other business methods, including particularly that of " the employment of one group by another," would similarly give cause for question.

The first part of the discussion now to follow will accordingly bear on the possible attitude of the Society to various business habits, in particular the two mentioned here. This will be a fairly extensive task. Later it will be necessary to consider more personal economic matters, such as the attitude to property and inheritance.

Competition.

In confronting the problem of competition, the

members of the Society would need to determine, at
the outset, whether they would be justified in engaging
at all in the process of competition. They would have
to decide the broad ethical problem, whether competition is or is not intrinsically wrong.

It was suggested earlier that some degree of competition is inevitable in any régime which aims at
high efficiency; and in so far as it is indispensable to
the attainment of this approved end, it may be claimed
as virtuous unless on other grounds it shows itself to
be wrong. Further, it was said, the term embraces
two different concepts : the act of competition, and
the spirit of competition. Once the distinction is
drawn between these two things it becomes immediately evident that there can be nothing ethical or
unethical about the competitive act. This is simply
a form of measurement necessary to compare two
individuals or two units. It is an essential element
in any system which has " maximum contribution "
in view; for only by competitive measurement is it
possible to discover the efficient workers and give them
their due responsibility.

If, therefore, acts of competition are necessary as
instruments of efficiency, not only would society as a
whole be wrong in attempting to avoid them entirely,
but the individual would also be wrong if he were to
refuse at all times to take part in them. As far as the
individual competitor is concerned, there can be no
degradation, but only test and strengthening, if each

competitive act is regarded by him as what it should be—a means of enabling society to make corporately its "maximum contribution."

But this does not solve the whole problem. It may be true that some degree of competition is inevitable : and it may be obvious that advantages are to be gained from it which can be gained in no other way : nevertheless, a method which is good in moderation is not always good beyond a certain stage. Moreover, it may happen that, in some spheres, although competition might seem desirable to permit the selection of the most efficient producers, yet, when applied, it fails, in fact, to bring forward the ablest. Often the most astute competitor, rather than the most constructive, secures the advantage. And there may even be parts of industry in which any producer who refuses to follow the practices of the more astute will be forced from the market altogether. Hence, the essential question is : In what spheres, and subject to what restrictions, may competition suitably be used ?

The section of industry in which competition as now applied produces most general dissatisfaction is that of commerce. In this sphere every person engaged is virtually driven to follow whatever may be the market's conventional methods. Throughout the merchanting and competitive freight system all trade is done on exceedingly small margins. Profit for the merchant is derived solely from the fractional difference between the buying price and the selling price, and depends, more than on any other factor, on the capacity to drive hard bargains and let no chance slip. The chance which is most significant is that which offers when some customer or producer is in peculiar difficulty; if he is already being driven to the wall, this is the time when he can be squeezed most firmly. Not to squeeze is to lose profit; to lose profit is to sink in the competition. Hence all competitors must be adamant in their attempt to grind down others if they wish to survive themselves.

Moreover, in the driving of a bargain there is advantage both in having knowledge and in the power to conceal. If a trader's situation is precisely known, and if he in turn can be kept in ignorance of the opposing strength, he can be pressed to his last concession. Success comes first, then, to those whose skill is of the type required, say, for poker; and whoever plays with cards on the table will play only till he loses all, which will not be long.

The position as thus described is perhaps not representative; but those who should know best seem to be agreed that in commerce there are many tracts in which it is impossible to apply any ethics whatever except, perhaps, those appropriate to a form of guerilla warfare. It would be indeed difficult, therefore, for the members of the Society to decide what they would do in this sphere.

The problem is one which affects both employers

and employees, the one being sometimes only the tool of the other. Possibly the difficulty is greater for the employee, since, for the time being, he is not master of his fate. He can make no radical change of methods, being himself under orders; and he risks dismissal if at any time he shows independence. Thus, when required in business to represent inexactly, or to mislead customers, or when pressed to gain information illicitly about competitors, the only alternatives for him are compliance or loss of work.

The problem which all such difficulties raise for an experimental group is, in essence, that of deciding whether they might justifiably follow the simple course of deserting every type of competitive employment which failed to lend itself to their principle. The objection to such a course would be that it would in reality mean running away from the very problem they had set forth to solve. Clearly, as far as the individual is concerned, he will have found an adequate solution to his personal problem once he has secured work in industry which conforms to the Society's approved code. But this brings no gain in general principle. Rather it defeats principle; for when competition for unsavoury posts is reduced, they become more lucrative for those who take them without qualm.

Possibly no real desertion is involved in such a running-away policy, if, in the case of each industrial process avoided, it can be said : Given a different type of organisation, and given *enough* contributive persons to work the organisation, the process could be run to the taste of everyone. Were the Society to adopt such an attitude, it would merely be admitting that things which may be possible to twenty thousand are not always possible to twenty; and its position would seem sound if it could actively survive in a considerable part of industry, whilst showing that the remainder could be run according to its principle as soon as there were sufficient numbers demanding change.

There are, indeed, large expanses of industry in which profit depends on efficiency, and in which unquestioned ethics are no handicap. Throughout the whole of the manufacturing and extractive industries, for instance, the power to gain the confidence of customers for reliableness and quality is indispensable to any large success. In this highly complex constructive section of industry, as well as in many of the professions and in that part of retailing which involves taste or good management, the contributive person must almost inevitably win. Here the requirements are : real concern in the work; a faculty for organising; capacity to draw the co-operation of other men; understanding of customers' needs; and vision. Whoever makes a religion of his service must inevitably succeed in this sphere.

If in the remainder of competitive industry, including some sections of merchanting, transport, land agency, and building, there are to be found branches here and there in which it is impossible to survive without adopting a dubious code, it seems fair to say that it is precisely in these parts that the competition is most wasteful and could with most advantage be supplemented by the Cartel system or by State ownership.

There would be immense economic gain, for example, from State control of land. A vast army of agents and solicitors would be released for other work; rent increases would accrue to the State; transport lines could be built straight; mines would be exploited from suitable positions; the speculative builder would be fettered; and natural beauty would be at least in some degree respected.

As regards transport, important economies not attainable under competition can be realised from a restricted monopoly, the chief gain being the avoidance of cross-freights.

In the case of the marketing of materials, at present accompanied by much waste and speculation, German experience seems to point to special advantages arising from the Cartel system—a method of organisation under which substantially all the output of an industry is sold by one agency.

Thus, if the Contributive Society were to avoid certain of the competitive zones in which the members could not easily survive, they would probably find that these zones were precisely the parts which yield

M

the worst social results under competition; and they
would be justified in such cases in working indirectly
for a change of organisation, rather than in striving
to adjust themselves individually, by compromise, to
the existing competitive organisation.

It might not in practice always be easy for a member
of the Society to change his occupation in order to
escape work not approved, especially in the case of an
employee. In a country where labour is extremely
mobile, and new openings are constantly being made
through industrial growth, the difficulty is less serious.
Thus, the situation in America or the Dominions,
where these conditions largely prevail, is widely
different from that of Great Britain. In this country,
burdened with continuous unemployment, no man can
afford easily to lose his existing work, lest he should
find no other. In the case of a man with family
responsibilities, the risk of being without employment
for months and possibly years consecutively is one
which few can contemplate.

This kind of dilemma facing the employed person is
itself perhaps the strongest evidence of the necessity
for the formation of a definite Society, an organisation
for mutual support, as opposed to a sprinkling of
scattered individuals each attempting to work out a
separate solution. For whereas men are often unable
single-handed to meet a situation, jointly they may
succeed. In the case of the Contributive Society, for
instance, it may be assumed that the membership

would at first comprise at least a few employers, and that these would be able to offer work, in cases of extreme difficulty, to the employee members. The guarantee which this would provide would have the incidental advantage of enabling members to uphold the Society's aims and views more vigorously before dismissal.

Apart from the purely ethical question, just discussed, there arises in connection with competition an essentially economic problem—namely, that of attaining maximum efficiency in production. If the economic system as a whole is to be judged from the point of view of "maximum contribution," then every separate feature in the system must similarly be judged by this criterion. It is pertinent, therefore, to discuss whether competition, as a method, in all instances would lead to greater efficiency than, say, State monopoly or some form of private co-operation.

There are numerous industries in which competition has already been supplanted or modified by monopolistic control, and others in which the tendency is strongly towards monopoly. The aim of the change in almost all cases has been to achieve greater efficiency; and it is improbable that the change would have taken place if, in any case, a serious sacrifice of production had been involved.

One problem confronting the Contributive Society would thus be to decide whether the industries in which the members were engaged were of such a nature as to be most efficiently organised on a competitive or a non-competitive basis. In reality, this would be, not one, but a multitude of problems, since each industry would need to be considered separately.

The industries which are most suitable for national-isation are those which provide essential public services; tend ordinarily towards monopoly (*e.g.* are subject to the law of increasing returns); involve no great risk; yield services or goods which admit of standardisation in quality; have a stereotyped form of administration; raise no serious problem of discipline; do not throw the Governments of different countries into economic conflict with one another; and lend themselves to arbitrary price-fixing and wage-fixing. The industries which are least suitable for nationalisation are those which fail signally to satisfy the above criteria, or which require artistic taste in either the producer or the consumer. Whenever æsthetic judgment, whim, fashion, or independent choice on the part of the customer is involved, he will inevitably be best served if there are innumerable units vying for patronage. Thus the occupations which will be among the last to be considered for public control will be : most professions; decorating industries, building, furnishing, painting, tailoring; printing and publishing; the production of instruments and machines; and certain sections of retailing.

It is evident, in view of the large number of con-

siderations involved, that for most industries the
decision as to the most suitable form of organisation
will be exceedingly difficult to make. Moreover,
whether the general view is in favour of or against
monopoly, the process or reorganisation can be only
gradual. Thus the members of the Society could not
expect to be effective in bringing about extensive or
immediate change in any sphere. Nevertheless, at all
times, and in all industries, there is a trend; and it
would be the task of the members to reach some
decision as to the most beneficial trend in any sphere
in which they had influence, and lean accordingly.

There remains a final question in connection with
competition. In some particular industries it may be
decided definitely that the highest efficiency is to be
reached through the competitive method, and that,
therefore, this method should be continued. On
further examination, however, it may become evident
that still greater efficiency is to be gained if the *rules*
of competition are modified. For instance, under the
present accepted rules of competition every firm acts
in whatever manner will lead to its own maximum
profit, irrespective of whether this is to the advantage
of the community in general. If a restriction of output will be to the firm's advantage, it will in general
effect the restriction. If it can gain by patenting
inventions or by preserving secrecy as to its methods,
it will deny the rest of the industry the power to use

these, although their wider use might lead to much improvement in the whole industry's technique. Clearly, then, the ordinary competitive rule does not always lead to the highest contribution to society as a whole; and the question arises whether any modification of the rule may be possible. For the members of the Society the problem, in essence, would be that of deciding whether they could afford to place their own inventions and discoveries at the disposal of competitors.

The difficulties inherent in this proposal are evident. If one firm alone were to adopt a generous policy with its discoveries, it would thereby assume a considerable handicap. Inventions are not produced, and discoveries are not made, without much attendant expense. There is the cost of providing research facilities in the case of technical improvements, and there is the cost of rewarding inventors and offering inducements for employees in general to bring forward new suggestions. If any firm incurs these expenses and then at once places the results at the disposal of competitors, without any corresponding return, it may be defeated by its own generosity.

Clearly the counsel of perfection in such cases would be to secure some arrangement under which all firms in the industry would pool their information, at a fair price to each firm for its expense, and would combine in the promotion of research. One measure which might suitably be attempted would be the setting up of a Research Board for the whole industry, possibly under the ægis of the Government, the task of the Board being to evolve new methods of production and estimate their cost, to work out schemes of scientific management applicable to the particular industry, to collect statistical and other information, and to supply all such information to the subscribing firms. The Board might in addition purchase from individual firms the right of use of their separate discoveries, and communicate regular accounts of these to the remainder of its membership.[1]

Wherever such a system of reciprocity showed itself to be impracticable, the position in the industry would be again that in which each firm would stand alone; and each firm would have to decide independently what it would do with its own inventions. A reasonable policy for a firm in this situation would seem to be to retain all inventions under patent at least until they had paid their initial cost of production. Beyond that point they might be used to enable the firm to reduce its prices or give better value to the consumer, and thus expand its enterprise. And finally, when the firm had reached its maximum manageable size, it might facilitate the extension of its discoveries to the rest of the industry.

The more fully the question of competition is

[1] It appears that there is a precedent for this suggestion in the Research Board of the British Canning Industry.

examined, the more difficult does it appear to be to lay down any universal practical rules for the guidance of the would-be contributor. The aim to be attained is clear—the maximum benefit to society as a whole—but the method of attaining it seems to vary for each individual case.

The attitude here has been broadly this. Competition itself is in general advantageous. It provides the means whereby men of different qualities may be appointed to posts involving different responsibilities. And it excludes inefficient firms from production. It may, however, be carried to excess, or misapplied. The task of those whose aim is contribution is to limit the use of the competitive system to those spheres in which its virtues outweigh its disadvantages; and to secure for society the fullest possible gain from this method wherever it is, in fact, applied.

This may involve action by the individual both with regard to his personal conduct and to his influence upon general trends. It would seem desirable that, in the first place, the individual should personally avoid those sections of competitive industry in which ethics are a handicap, and that in other spheres, he should attempt so to modify competitive rules that the widest interests of the community may receive first consideration.

Apart from this there arises the necessity for seeking enlightenment at all times as to the causes underlying any general tendency in industry towards or away from monopoly, and for adding whatever influence seems possible to the most beneficial trend.

Individual Enterprise.

Whatever may have been the effect of the industrial revolution upon twentieth-century urban and rural life, this effect has been produced rather by the accumulated actions of separate individuals than by corporate enterprise. If towns have grown to vast and unwieldy proportions, it is because men in their ones and twos have decided to congregate. If dwellers in the centre of the cities have been cut off from the open fields, it is because single families have settled around the fringe. Slums have been created and intensified through the action of individual firms forcing their way into already crowded areas. Open spaces have been swallowed up by hosts of little builders each bent on his individual profit. The beauty of the country has been destroyed through the sacrifice of the occasional oak or the intrusion of the occasional bungalow. Wholesale devastation is a rare occurrence; otherwise the process might have met with opposition. As it is, life is being stifled by a kind of creeping disease, caused by the unthinking acts of millions of little people.

The position reached now seems to be one of almost complete anarchy. Each person adds his smudge wherever he will; and there seems to be no thought of achieving a higher liberty through some form of con-

trol. Military huts invade ancient ruins. Aeroplanes,
tanks, and lovers share the seclusion of the same
moors. Lands that should be the wanderer's refuge
swarm with vehicles. Even the highest peak in
America can be climbed by car! The whole world,
indeed, seems to be organising so that men may sit
sleekly among cushions and crowd on Nature; whilst
Nature's own people, seeking retreat, are driven even
further to find quietude in which to speak with her.
Why, one wonders, have we not the social sense to build
each a separate sanctuary : one for business, one for
homes; one for tramps, one for motors; one for
bathers, one for boat-craft; one for noise, one
for silence ?

Doubtless, amongst the " common purposes " of
the Society there would figure the aim of producing· a
greater social consciousness and order—the aim of
actively protecting the people as a whole against
people as individuals. But such a policy would take
many years to develop; and in the meantime the
members of the Society would have to evolve certain
rules for governing their own individual conduct :
to ensure that they were not inadvertently scattering
blots. The rules would not be easy to evolve; but
presumably they would be concerned mainly with the
precautions each individual should take in the choice
of business and housing sites; the prevention of smoke;
the avoidance of factory dirt and noise; and in the
consideration of questions of industrial architecture.

Relations between Employers and Employees.

In the analysis made earlier of the economic system, two " habits of conduct " were singled out as giving rise, more than any others, to moral issues. The first of these has already been discussed : the habit of " competition." The second is " the employment of one group by another." It is around these habits that the clash of interests between one employer and another, and between employers and workers, mainly turns; and for this reason they would be the object of special concern to the Society when business principles were being discussed.

In the case of " the employment of one group by another," it seems probable that in a perfect state this habit would itself virtually disappear. It will be seen later that the Contributive Society's principles, universalised, would yield a situation in which all would be employing all. Each person would become both employer and employed. But the situation to be considered at this initial stage is different. It is one in which the employer is assumed to be contributive, whilst engaging a large number of men, the majority of whom are acquisitive. The converse case of a contributive employee working for an acquisitive employer is to be considered later. At present attention is being confined to employers' principles.

The criterion which the employer would use in

determining his relations with workers may be assumed
to be, as before, the necessity for maximising his
direct and indirect contribution. Since the power
of service of an employer is mainly indirect, depending
essentially on the capacity to induce others to strive,
the chief problem of a member of the Society in this
position is to advance his philosophy in the eyes of
those associated with him. In essence, the task is
to render the firm itself, as a comprehensive unit,
as fully contributive as possible. To this end the
most desirable thing would be, again, to set a fashion.
For a fashion taken up by large companies of men
would be of profoundly greater influence than the
single effort or profits of the employer. Thus in all
relations with the staff the employer would have one
chief thought in mind : to induce them to see his
particular light.

In setting this as the aim, the employer considered
here starts from a position of special strength. He
may be drawing very substantial profits. But he
spends personally something equivalent to an average
wage. That is, he lives at about the same level as
the men who do the mechanical work of his factory.
His home is of the same standard as theirs, and is
probably in the same district. His surplus earnings
are spent on the " common purposes " and other
social services. Hence whatever contributive ideas
he might wish to launch they would at least be loaded
with the weight of illustration.

If, then, the main thought of the employer is to develop in his group a certain general outlook and motive, the first step towards such an end must be to make them self-determining. One cannot put virtue into an automaton. To acquire any quality whatever, a person must have the power of choice. And if the aim is to produce a general contributive volition, the first indispensable condition is that each individual shall be able to express volition. At the outset, therefore, the employer would presumably proceed to give those engaged with him a definite voice in their own doings. He would attempt to provide channels through which each individual might express, on any point whatever, his view or wish.

The initial development towards this position—though by itself it probably would not carry far—might be the establishment of a Works Council. Such a Council, being representative of every important grade in the firm, might be consulted regularly by the management on all matters affecting the workers' interests : conditions of employment and discharge, works regulations, welfare and educational facilities, and opportunities for promotion.

A further move might be the introduction of schemes for the encouragement of invention, so that all members of the firm might gain not only a sympathetic, but an eager hearing when they had a suggestion to bring forward, and receive their due equivalent.

By far the most important step, however, would be the establishment of a system of co-ownership. By this is meant a scheme under which the employees possess a considerable share of a firm's capital, and have a voice in its actual management. A share in control, based on definite ownership, is without question the most effective means of creating the condition of self-determination in all ranks. Moreover, it couples this new liberty with the assumption of responsibility. Each individual employee has a personal stake in his unit; he shares both the privilege and the obligation of directing its policy towards appropriate ends.

The ideal situation would seem to have been reached by the Columbia Conserve Company of Indianapolis, under the presidency of William P. Hapgood. A beginning was made in this Company in 1917 by the appointment of a Works Council. Through the medium of the Council the workers take part in determining their own wages, hours, and conditions of work and the general policies of the business. The system of co-ownership was established at an early stage, and is progressive in its effect of transferring control to the workers. " Out of the profits of the business 7 per cent. is first paid on the preferred stock. Out of the remaining profits a cumulative dividend of 10 per cent. is paid on the common stock and the same percentage to the workers on their pay-roll. Ten per cent. of the remainder is then set aside for a pension fund. All the remaining profit goes to the employees as a group, being used to buy outstanding common stock. This stock is held by the council in a trust fund, the workers receiving the dividends from the stock. The ownership of the business will pass into the hands of the council when they have purchased 51 per cent. of the common stock." [1]

The aim of this company has been to create a condition of effective self-government in industry, whilst avoiding paternalism. It appears to have succeeded. But this does not signify that the original director of the company has in any sense lost his influence as a contributor, or has in the long run diminished his profits. From a purely formal point of view he may seem to have sacrificed his power, since he has even resigned from the chairmanship of the Council, lest he should tend to overawe the other members. But the real test of the power is whether the ideas originally conceived in the mind of the director have become the ideas of his co-workers. If the workers are, in fact, carrying out vigorously the policies and aims with which he started, as is so in this case, then his power is supreme in that it has already accomplished all that he desired.

Similarly, if an employer in the Society had a mind to sow ideas amongst his group, he would assuredly not expect success from the exercise of

[1] Sherwood Eddy, *Religion and Social Justice.* Doran, New York.

financial control, but only from the force of the ideas themselves. Ultimately, external compulsion is powerless : movement and change come only from intellectual persuasion. The method to be followed in the implanting of any new attitude would thus seem to be, first, to introduce a condition of self-government, and secondly, to develop the atmosphere and general situation in which the new ideas may spring.

As just observed, the employer would individually be well placed for sowing his Society's particular seed. He might become more effective, however, through the adoption of certain aids. The intention, broadly stated, would be to set a fashion under which all might become alert to make their firm an effective communal service. To this end several ways of action might be suggested. One would be to press for a system under which part of the profits would be distributed beyond the limits of the concern itself. A grant might be made, for instance, to support a Research Board of the type described earlier. The national trade union might be subsidised for the purpose of collecting labour statistics and providing special educational facilities. In addition, something would be gained by assisting local social services directly out of the profits of the firm. Suggestions might be invited from employees as to the particular services they would wish to aid, so that a list might be drawn up representing their own initiative and will.

A further method of enabling those engaged to realise something of the "service" aspect of their efforts would be to bring customers as often as possible into direct touch with the actual producers, the men tending the machines, and the draughtsmen responsible for designs, and to invite comments both adverse and favourable.

There is little new in these suggestions; in fact, most of them are already applied in one unit or another. The point of their interest here, however, lies in the fact that, given the conditions in which they are applied, they can be used to a specific end; they may serve as a basis of suggestion to prompt into being certain desired ways of viewing the daily function of the individual and of the firm. In their special context, these measures may become part of a general process whereby the author of the system secures the acceptance of his criteria by the main body of the firm.

The key-note of the suggestions made here is the need for attempting to create a tradition. Manifestly, the ideal situation to be achieved in industry is one in which the members of each productive unit, as a body, aim at contribution. But towards this end there is no simple and infallible way of approach; and any suggestions offered as to possible ways can be little more than illustrative.

The difficulty involved in the achievement of the

N

aim is evident, if only from the fact that the aim, though advanced repeatedly by socialist or idealist movements, has rarely been reached. It represents, for instance, the core of the Rotary principle. And in spite of the large number of the adherents of this principle, probably few would claim that it was effective throughout their concerns.

One of the chief difficulties confronting any wide advance towards the contributive outlook is the existence of the " joint stock " organisation of industry. Many firms are owned, not by single employers, but by hundreds of shareholders; and as a consequence the entire policy of the firms tends to be governed by the urge for high dividends. The power of any single individual to modify the attitude of a complete unit to its productive task, even though he may be in a key position, is slight.

A second main difficulty is that many of the conditions under which a firm works are imposed on it from without, either by employers' regulations or by trade unions, or by joint national agreements. In some cases these regulations oppose any attempt at maximum contribution by restricting output per man or per firm. And they sometimes directly or indirectly impede co-operation within a firm by discouraging the adoption of co-partnership schemes.

Given the wide variation in the difficulty confronting different employers, it seems that, from the point of view of a contributive society, it would be impossible to lay down precise rules as to the attitude of employer members to their employees. The general trend desired would be towards the setting of a fashion, among the staff and associates, based on the Society's criteria. And towards this end certain broad lines of action might be suggested : the creation among all ranks of freedom of choice and self-government; the development of ownership-sharing; and the recognition of ownership itself as a trust or opportunity for social homage.

Wage-earning and Salaried Persons.

It frequently happens, in consequence of the size and complexity of business enterprise, that the responsibility for policy rests as much on employees as on employers. In fact, whoever chances to be most competent in the hierarchy of control, whether he be nominally in charge or not, usually carries the main burden of responsibility for decisions. In these circumstances the situation of employees may be closely similar to that of employers, and their problems may be much alike.

The large majority of employees are, however, in situations involving little control over policy, and they therefore have no opening for constructive work apart from their immediate tasks. If they desire to express ingenuity and initiative it must be mainly in the pursuit of aims attainable only through spare time activity. And although these are innumerable, varied, and of profound importance, they do not seem to raise difficulties of principle, such as are found in industry. At the present stage the chief concern is with problems which arise in the course of trade or professional work.

It sometimes happens that a highly contributive person, say, a social worker, or a teacher doing pioneer work in education, or a minister of religion, feels that his principles demand of him that he should receive less salary than is currently paid for his class of work, and that, were all men to hold similar principles, they would universally be contented with payment equal to the average wage.

There appear to be two main grounds on which this attitude may be questioned. In the first place, the matter of real concern is, not how much a person receives, but how much he spends on his own gratification. If he restricts his own expenditure to the average wage, then the higher his income is the better; for all the surplus will be spent socially. It is evident, for instance, that, in the case of the Contributive Society, each member would be anxious to earn all he could in order to have an ample surplus for the " common purposes " ; and the more he could earn, the more would the purposes prosper. A high income in this case is all gain. In the second place, it is important from the point of view of comparing the efficiency of different units that all persons employed should be paid a wage or a salary corresponding to their relative efficiency as producers. Unless the wages paid reflect the efficiency of the workers, it is impossible to make an accurate comparison of real labour costs, and therefore impossible to determine which units in industry should be expanded and which closed down.

Hence, an employee would at all times be justified from the broader economic standpoint in accepting and, if necessary, pressing for payment which equalled his value as a producer. In the estimate of productive worth, due regard would be paid to the amount which he could earn in other occupations.

A second problem arises, not so much in connection with the amount of income received, but with respect to service given directly, through trade or profession, to society. There may be contributive employees who are anxious to increase their direct gift of service to others, but find themselves impeded through a certain twist of circumstances : the fact that they are primarily the servants of some single individual or small group, and not of the wider community. Thus, however they may exert themselves, the fruits of their efforts will be harvested solely by their immediate employer. Moreover, if this employer is of the self-interested type, their efforts will be worse than wasted; by swelling his profits they will tend to aggravate an existing evil : the disparity between the incomes of different classes. In such circumstances, therefore, they feel little disposed to expend more energy than is just necessary to ensure their being continuously employed.

This method of reasoning seems, however, to be based on a somewhat restricted view. It may be true that if one individual alone increases his productive effort the employer will probably benefit. But if a large number of workers distributed over an industry were to do so, consumers, rather than employers, would ultimately gain. The first effect of the greater productive effort might be an increase of profits. But later, when the additional product began to press upon the market and lead to a decline of prices, the advantage would be transferred to the consumer.

If a still wider view of the situation is taken, and the assumption is made that productive effort increases over the whole of industry, there can be no question that this would bring benefit to all members of the community, including wage-earners. It is a commonplace of statistics that whenever there is a general improvement in the efficiency of industry, no matter how this may originate, the advantage ultimately spreads itself in certain scarcely alterable proportions throughout the different economic classes.

The question arises, then, whether it is sounder for an employee to regard himself as a single individual whose extra effort will react solely to the advantage of his immediate employer, or to regard himself as a

member of a large group, influencing and being
influenced by others. The answer must to some
extent depend upon the individual, and his position
as a member of the group.

In general, the rule towards which employee mem
bers of the Society would probably be drawn, on the
basis of their contributive principle, might be summarised thus : When possible, to secure an increase
of earnings for any increase of efficiency and use the
surplus socially; and when this is not possible, to
fill their quota of work steadily without much consideration for where the benefit might fall. In any
event, it would be within nobody's power to determine what the final reactions of any effort would,
in fact, be.

The Disposal of Property.

It may be recalled that it is not the wish in this
chapter to state an opinion on what ought, morally,
to be. The aim is to show what would, in fact,
happen, if action were widely governed by a certain
motive. It is true that, if it becomes evident that
the universalising of this motive would lead to results
which are much desired, then it may be said as a
corollary that it is a duty to attempt to acquire the
motive. But, apart from this, the concern here is
with fact and deduction, rather than with obligation.
The assumption having first been made that there

exist persons with a contributive drive, it remains
to discover, not how they should, but how they
would, act.

Thus, at the present stage, when action with regard
to " property " is being discussed, the concern is to
know, not what they ought to do with their property,
but what they would do with it if they were bent on
pressing it into service most effectively.

The situation envisaged is that of a group of persons who, after limiting their personal expenditure
to an amount in the neighbourhood of the average
wage, have a surplus of income and savings to pool
for use towards the " common purposes." The
essence of the problem before each member would
be to decide what amount of the surplus he might
place in the keeping of the Society, for corporate
holding, and for promoting the approved purposes.

Prima facie it would seem that at least some
increase in the efficiency of use of the surplus would
be gained from corporate ownership and administration. Whenever a number of persons find that they
have like interests and that the service of these
interests costs money, time, and organisation, all will
become more effective in their quest if they join forces
and to some extent pool their means. In the case of
extensive projects, especially, financial co-operation
would seem to be a *sine quâ non* of success.

The question of chief interest, however, is : What
precise proportion of their surplus would the members

retain in their own hands; and what proportion
would they hand over to the Society? Quite clearly
they would need to retain a certain amount of their
excess earnings for personal disposal. After spending the equivalent of the average wage for their
own upkeep and needs, they would still require some
small further amount for personal business expenses,
such as travel, stationery, or publications entailed in
the process of work. They would require something
for private donations and for the support of religious
and political aims. And they might have certain
social responsibilities which could not readily be
entrusted to the care of an impersonal group or committee. In all such cases it is evident that there
could be no other satisfactory method of spending
the money than privately, and that the members
would retain such part of their surplus earnings as
they needed for these purposes.

As regards past earnings, saved and invested as
capital, there might similarly be advantage in retaining a certain proportion in private hands. The objection to pooling capital irrevocably in a society is
that it cannot thereafter be transferred to a use not
covered by the society's rules and aims. Thus if a
member felt that he might at some time need part
of his past savings, say, to assist him in a political
career, or towards the building of a church, he would
not tie up the whole of his capital in the hands of a
society which did not comprise these aims. In fact

it is unlikely that any member would hand over a substantial proportion of his wealth irrevocably to the Society until he had reached that stage in life at which he could forecast with some certainty the trend of his future interests.

If this is so, it follows that the members would lay down no hard-and-fast rule as to the proportion to be transferred to the Society, either of surplus current earnings, or of past earnings. The amount to be pooled would be left to the discretion of each individual.

With this reservation, it seems probable, however, that the members would be disposed to place in the keeping of the Society as much as they could—that is, they would take risks in the direction of pooling too much rather than too little.

There are several reasons for such a belief. In the first place, if it is desired to promote any object whatever, regularly and continuously, this is as a rule possible only through the formation of a fund for the purpose, a fund to which different persons contribute by subscription outright. The fund is then placed in the trusteeship of some body established to administer it. In the case of the Contributive Society, formed specifically to promote certain social aims—*i.e.* the accepted " common purposes "—definite endowment would probably be indispensable for the promotion of some of the purposes selected. Unless the Society could be assured of a regular income from property owned by itself, it would be much limited in its range of social services.

For this reason alone the members would probably be disposed to contribute as much as they could by donation to the common fund. But, in so far as they were to follow such a policy, they would realise several additional gains. One of these is that capital which is centralised for administration becomes increasingly safe. Whereas losses which may accrue to a single small capitalist will mean a serious handicap to him and to any schemes he may have in hand, a large corporate holder of capital, being able to make numerous investments and spread risks, will be insured against such losses. A reserve will be built up from gains on strong investments to meet any losses on others, and the security of the whole will become virtually absolute.

More important than this economic gain, perhaps, is the psychological advantage which results when members of a society find themselves able to pool their possessions. Anyone who succeeds in divesting himself of substantially all his property discovers thereby an extraordinary sense of freedom. It gives him assurance that he has been able, once and for all, to put the acquisitive motive in its place; and it yields a sense of victory and an absence of mental obsession from which a completely sane view of property can be developed. Moreover, the same gesture may have a similar effect, by contagion, on the outlook of others who are possessed by the current attitude to property. When any outlook is clearly unsound, it is only necessary to place the true outlook side by side with it to set the remedy in motion.

The chief gain in principle, however, from the pooling of property is that it automatically means a renunciation of the right of inheritance. Whoever hands over his possessions to a society or trust thereby forgoes the power to pass on wealth to a succession of heirs. To break from the inheritance right in this way has a far-reaching implication. For, as noted earlier, the handing down of wealth from heir to heir has two vitally important economic effects. In the first place, it causes capital and income to accumulate snowball-fashion and become concentrated in the hands of the few. Secondly, by so doing it places the control of industry and immense social power in the hands of these few persons, who are selected, not because they have shown efficiency in business or a high social philosophy, but by the fortune of birth.

It seems that a person who was bent on maximising his contribution, both present and future, would be anxious to dispose of his property so that in future generations it would be controlled in industry by persons of tried efficiency, and so that the income from it would be devoted throughout to the most urgent needs. Thus it may be assumed that the members of the Society would as far as possible place their capital in its corporate ownership, and so draft the rules of

the Society that the capital and income from it would
be most efficiently used in industry and in social
service.

This would not signify that no provision would be
made for sons and heirs; but whereas the principle
of inheritance often has the effect now of causing
dependents to expect, from early life onwards, to
become parasitic on others' wealth, and thus destroys
even the prospect of their acquiring self-dependence,
the provision made by a member of the Society would
presumably be such as to enable his successors to
become independently contributive. Effective education and an opening for work would be among the
chief features of the assistance.

The general finding with regard to the ownership
of property would thus seem to be along the following
lines. In essence, it would be of not the slightest
concern to the members in what form of legal ownership their earnings were held, provided that, in the
application of the earnings, the most effective results
were gained. The matter of legal possession is superficial; the method of application fundamental; hence
the nature of the possession would be determined by
the nature of the desired application. To the extent
that capital and income were needed for their more
symbolic uses, for the more intimate types of social
service, or for religious or political interests, they
would tend to be retained in private hands. To the

extent that they were needed for social uses capable of being most effectively promoted through a corporate body, they would be pooled in a common fund.

It may be expected that the members, in pooling their surplus income or capital, would stipulate the direction in which the property thus given should be applied. That is, although the property would come into the legal ownership of the Society, each donor, as a member of the Society, would individually determine the direction in which his own donation would be applied.

As regards inheritance, it seems probable that, after making " average " provision for dependents, members would by will or otherwise ensure the transfer of any remaining capital to the Society or other trust.

The Administration of Funds.

The Society, on receiving property from members, would have two chief tasks to perform : first, to secure the highest possible income from the capital transferred to it ; secondly, to apply its income effectively towards the accepted " common purposes." For these main tasks it might find it advisable to set up two separate Departments, an Investing Department and a Social Services Department.

The Investing Department would then receive all contributions, whether of income or capital, from members, and would endeavour to place them in

industry in investments which seemed most beneficial from the wider point of view of the Society.
Frequently the most profitable method of using the
capital would be to lend it to members of the Society
who showed promise as managers, to enable them to
set up in business or to extend. Any member assisted
thus would stand in much the same relation to the
Investing Department as the Managing Director
stands to a Board of Directors. And the Department
itself might in course of time develop into a " holding
company," having a controlling influence over a
considerable number of firms.

The Social Services Department would concern
itself solely with the distribution of the Society's
income amongst the objects comprised in the " common purposes." Its directors would include the most
qualified administrators among the members, and its
mode of organisation would presumably be similar
to that of an ordinary charitable trust at the present
time.

Security and Insurance.

One of the gains from the retention of property in
private hands is that the property represents in itself
an insurance for the owner against all economic risks.
It is an insurance for him during his lifetime; and if
he can pass it on at death, it continues to provide
security and income for his wife and family and other
dependents.

It follows that if the Society allows members to transfer to it any substantial proportion of their wealth it should be prepared, in return, to protect them by some form of general insurance. A suitable method might be to establish some scheme whereby each member would have a claim on the Society up to the limit of his own contribution, if he should fall on evil days. That is, the Society might undertake to repay his contributions, in case of need, in weekly amounts corresponding to the "average wage," either to the member or to his dependents after his death.

Summary of the First Stage of Development.

It may be well to outline again here the salient features of the rules which the aim of "maximum contribution" would seem to impose on a group.

There are two main spheres to which the rules would apply : that of personal economic action, and that of business conduct. The outline given here may conveniently follow this division.

A. *Personal Economic Action.*

1. *Expenditure.*—Since the object of the contribution is to benefit the whole of society, no member of it being regarded as more significant than any other, the aim of "maximum contribution" would lead the contributor to adopt voluntarily the principle of sharing, or the "average wage." The only case in which this limit of expenditure would be exceeded would be

where an increase in personal outlay above the average wage would lead to an increase in the surplus rendered up to society.

2. *Property.*—As a result of the adoption of the "average wage," certain resources would be made available for social use. There would thus arise a "problem of property," or of the right disposal of the surplus earned. "Maximum contribution" would entail only that property should be held in such a way that it would yield most benefit, present and future. During early life much might be held in private hands, so that it might be transferred readily from use to use. Later it would tend to be committed progressively to the Society or to a permanent trust for social objects selected by the contributor.

3. *Inheritance.*—In so far as property was thus conveyed to the Society or a trust, this would mean a renunciation of the "right of inheritance."

4. *Insurance.*—Arising out of the receipt of property from members, the Society would have an obligation laid upon it to support the members in case of need. Some form of general insurance would be required, guaranteeing an "average wage" to contributors or their dependents.

B. *Business Conduct.*

In the sphere of industry, "maximum contribution" would seem to involve :

1. The avoidance of socially harmful trades.

o

2. The preservation of competition wherever competitive measurement is required for raising efficient persons to responsible positions, or for removing less efficient units, or where rival production would tend to give the greatest variety and personal satisfaction to consumers.

3. The attempt to apply co-operative methods wherever competition has unsatisfactory net effects.

4. In industrial relations, the attempt to arrive at a position in which all persons share the ownership of, and the responsibility for, industry; and the creation of an attitude to production such that each business unit, as a body, becomes a public service.

It is evident that whereas the first group above, comprising personal economic principles, would be capable of application by individuals immediately and completely, the second group, business principles, could be applied only to a limited extent by men in their ones and twos. These business principles suggest a possible directive, a line of development, the consummation of which would depend on the growth in number of persons desiring their adoption.

In reality, the widespread application of the personal rules would in course of time lead to the attainment of the desired business principles; hence, whoever followed such rules fully would have the satisfaction of knowing that he, individually, was a unit consistent with an ultimate completely contributive scheme.

THE SECOND STAGE OF DEVELOPMENT

The only important problem of extension to be considered so long as the Society does not grow beyond, say, one-twentieth of the whole population, is that of internal organisation. Its general economic reactions would up to that point be so slight that they may reasonably be neglected. Hence, in this second stage, attention may be confined exclusively to the problem of extending the Society's organisation to include larger numbers.

The first question which would arise as the membership increased would be the limit of size to which the parent Society might grow before decentralising into a series of small groups. Thereafter it would be necessary to determine the most suitable size for each of the groups.

The active cell, or unit, in all organisations is as a rule incomparably smaller than the general body of the organisation. Thus a church may have a million adherents, whilst the active unit is at the most a few hundred. A university may have several thousand members, whereas the departments or separate colleges work on the basis, again, of a few hundred. According to the nature of the activity involved, there will be an optimum size for the unit, a size from which variation is as a rule only possible or beneficial where there emerge peculiarly strong personalities capable of co-ordinating larger numbers. It may be said that the nature of the activity determines the *average* size of the unit, whereas personalities or combinations of personalities determine the *variations* from this average. This is broadly true of industrial, as well as of social and religious units.

As a further generalisation it may be said that, where the personal stake or interest in the success of the venture is great, the unit tends to be small. Thus, in industry, where a man's whole position and livelihood may depend on the profit derived, the average board of directors numbers less than twenty. The intensity of concern for success makes difficult the mutual adjustment of opinions of more than a small number of persons. Needless to say, where some exceptional personality arises there may be a wide variation from the average.

On the basis of these ideas it would seem that the average unit in the Contributive Society, once it had begun to decentralise, would be relatively small, probably not exceeding fifty. To each member, the Society would be both church and industry; it would engage the most vital interests of each. Co-operation in the pursuit of the Society's aims would thus tend to be on the basis of a high degree of compatibility of temperament, discoverable only among small groups.

Confirmation of the belief that the Society's active unit would be small is drawn from consideration of the *nature* of the decentralisation involved. Decentralisation would almost certainly be on the basis of function and aim. That is, there would be a division, in the first place, into Industrial Trusts and Social Service Trusts, absorbing respectively the functions of the Investing Department and the Social Service Department of the Society; and, in the second place, both the Industrial Trusts and the Social Service Trusts would probably confine themselves to promoting limited branches of business or social enterprise. Stated another way, this implies that individuals would only come together on the basis of the desire to pursue some limited, common aim. In some cases they would join forces to engage in certain trades; in other cases they would join in the pursuit of social ends. The groupings in all cases would tend to be fairly small, though perhaps larger in the case of the Social Service Trusts than the Industrial Trusts.

The position visualised in the "second stage" of the Society's growth is thus one in which there exist numerous separate, independent trusts, organised either on an industrial or on a social basis. The Social Service Trusts comprise persons who co-operate, on grounds of like philosophy, in promoting some particular enthusiasm : say, education, or new art, or research, or health reform, one such special aim being the essential co-ordinating link between the members, though not precluding other things. The income of the Social Service Trusts is drawn partly from the surplus earnings of the members and partly, perhaps, from endowments conveyed to them from the Industrial Trusts.

The Industrial Trusts are concerned more with earning than with spending, though their aim is to build up some branch or allied branches of industry so that funds might be yielded later for expenditure, either directly for communal ends, or through the Social Service Trusts. Their essential function is that of a " holding company " : to invest funds in industry; to control that part of industry in which their investments give them the governing influence; to appoint managers and staff; and, in general, to carry on the duties of a super-board of directors or financial trust.

Wherever decentralisation of this nature takes place in a movement which has a common philosophic basis, the decentralisation is invariably accompanied by some system of co-ordination. All parts of the movement are brought into association through a central administration. In the case now considered the need would inevitably arise for some powerful headquarters, or governing body, to maintain the Trusts in mutual contact.

Such a body might perhaps take the form of a Central Trust, having certain national services to control and, in particular, providing the basis of co-operation for the local Trusts. Its Board of Trustees, being the executive for the whole Society, would be responsible for organising the General Meetings, preparing the Agenda, and carrying into effect Resolutions. It would preserve association among the local Trusts, not only through enabling them to give expression to their combined will, but also through exchange of thought by means of correspondence and publications. It might be responsible, further, for maintaining contacts with other societies whose interests ran parallel with those of the Contributive Society.

In addition, the Central Trust would presumably undertake social activities of broad national importance. Thus whereas the local Trusts would be interested more especially in municipal development, the clearing of open spaces, the formation of clubs and evening classes, there would remain for the Central Trust such national services as educational experiment, scientific research, insurance, publicity, reform of penitentiaries, and the preservation of national monuments.

In order to perform these duties, the Central Trust would need to be heavily endowed with legacies and subscriptions from the local Trusts. The funds received would necessarily be invested in industry, but probably in shares carrying no managerial responsibility. The management of industry and all direct contacts with business life might perhaps with advantage be left to the more specialised local Industrial Trusts.

Financial Strength.

There remains one minor problem of organisation, namely, the limit of size to which local Trusts might be allowed to expand, financially, before effort was made to distribute their funds. It is conceivable that if, through legacies and the amassed earnings of previous members, a Trust were to become exceedingly powerful financially, new members would be drawn to join it through the power which membership would confer on them. Desire for power is a type of acquisitiveness more intense in some cases than the desire for luxury; and an excess of it is probably more harmful. Hence it would be unfortunate if the Society, merely through the inducement of its accumulated wealth, were to recruit into its ranks a large faction of power-seekers.

There would seem to be no hard-and-fast rule capable of dealing with this risk. It would be impossible, for instance, to fix a definite limit to the growth in size, financially, of the local Trusts. Each Trust would be legally self-determining, and its members would be unlikely to appreciate any reason for restricting their own growth at any given moment. The only limitation likely to be applied would be in the amount of " free legacies " passed down to new generations of trustees; and this would come, not by way of a generally imposed restriction, but because members, in passing over funds to the Trusts, would tend to define fairly precisely the manner in which the funds should be invested and applied. In other words, they would themselves exercise the main power yielded by the wealth, by determining at the outset the way in which the wealth should be used.

Such a policy, if generally applied by members, would have the effect of restricting the amount of the funds over which succeeding members would have discretionary control. In course of time the local Trusts might inherit vast sums of tied investments and endowments for specified objects, but much smaller sums for free use.

The Third Stage of Development

It is of little relevance for the actual thesis in these pages whether the contributive motive could, in fact, be generalised or whether the ideal régime shown on the basis of it could be attained. All that is needed is, as suggested earlier, to be able to outline a system such that it may be said " the *more nearly* this system is approached, the more fully will human purpose be achieved." The need is for the picture of a coherent system which, even though not attainable in the present—and possibly not in the future—will nevertheless act as guide to social development now.

In order to describe such a picture it is necessary to *assume* the generalisation of the contributive motive, and show what would happen if it were thus generalised.

There is another way in which it may be shown equally that it is not a criticism of any scheme to say that it could not be made universal. It would seem to be no adverse comment on Christianity, for instance, to show that, if followed rigidly by all persons, it would cancel out. For if humanity is unbalanced now, and if Christian conduct would yield an element of greater balance, then, for the time being this may be the ideal conduct.

Such an argument cannot be used here, however. The aim in this last section is to discover the character of a complete, ultimate system. To this end it is necessary to assume, theoretically, the universalising of some satisfying average motive, and to show that, when universalised, it would, in fact, be capable of producing a coherent system. The process itself may be purely theoretical; but it is needed in order to yield a practical result—namely, a concrete description of a system which, as far as can be judged, is the most satisfying objective of present effort and education.

The process to be followed here, then, is to re-examine the two groups of rules summarised at the end of the " first stage "—the rules of personal and business conduct derived from the contributive motive—and show what changes would take place in the economic system if the rules were universalised.

One chief effect would be upon the distribution of wealth and income. This may be considered here first, since most other changes in the system either directly result from the change in distribution, or are influenced by it.

The Distribution of Income.

Were all persons bent on maximum contribution, the national dividend would probably in a short time leap to twice the size it attains under acquisition. The " average wage " would be correspondingly high, and would probably be sufficient to meet all physical and cultural needs, so that only in the rarest instances would the principle of the average wage conflict with that of maximum contribution. In other words, no matter how delicate might be the work of the contributor concerned, the reduction of his expenditure to the average wage would mean no detriment to the work.

This assumption does not take into account, however, one important exception. There are some forms of contribution which can be made only *through expenditure*. It may be an æsthetic gift to society to wear rich clothing or to maintain some distinction in personal art or architecture. Were there no lavish expenditure of any kind, personal creative life would be much the poorer, and not only would those with talent lose power of expression, but there would be a much less range from which others could draw inspiration. Through the intermediary of the theatre, the Press, and the film, the life-art of every person becomes part of the life and beguilement of a wide community of others; and to narrow down the community's total range of expression is, in a very real sense, to narrow down the imaginative life of each member of it.

For the moment it will be necessary to pass over this exception and assume that, for the large majority, maximum contribution would lead to the adoption of the average wage. If this is assumed, it follows that in a community in which the motive of contribution was widespread, substantially all persons would be restraining their personal expenditure to this average and would pool their surplus for some united expression. Such action may be taken as the starting-point here for the discussion of income distribution.

On this basic assumption it is almost inevitable that there would emerge a new principle. In a completely contributive scheme, not only would persons earning high wages voluntarily limit themselves to their share, the average, but they would also insist that all persons should receive as much as their share. In other words, all wage-earners below the limit would receive a subsidy indirectly to make up their wages to the average. As noted earlier, for the efficient

working of an economic system it is desirable that
the wages paid in the first place by the employer
should correspond to the relative efficiency of the
worker. Thus, in a contributive régime direct wages
would probably continue to be related to efficiency,
but a subsidy would be given to persons earning low
wages, through either the State or the Society, to
bring their total income up to the average wage.

From this may be drawn the first point concerning
the *proportionate* distribution of income. Wages and
salaries at the present time amount to between 55
and 60 per cent. of the total National Income. Hence
in a system in which all were living at about the
average wage, and some had, in addition, a personal
outlay on religious or political aims, the amount of
personal expenditure of all kinds would be approximately 60 per cent. of the National Income.[1]

Rent, Interest, and Profit account for the remaining
40 per cent. Virtually the whole of this would accrue
to the Trusts : that is, the Industrial and Social
Service Trusts of the Society. For, as a consequence
of the perpetual handing over of funds by members
before death to the Society's keeping, the Society
would hold all past, accumulated capital. It would
own virtually all land and capital and enterprise,
and derive from them the corresponding Rent,
Interest, and Profit. The only property not held

---

[1] This percentage would, of course, become progressively greater as the
number of exceptions to the average wage rule, at present ignored, increased.

by the Trusts would be capital accumulated by members out of their surplus wages or salaries and not yet handed over to the Society, together with shares held by separate employed groups under co-partnership schemes.

As far as the *final* distribution of income is concerned, these exceptions to ownership do not matter; for, ultimately, the whole of the surplus 40 per cent. not spent privately would directly or indirectly be transferred to the Trusts. Every member making surplus earnings in industry would be a member of some Trust; and his surplus would be transferred to it sooner or later for social purposes selected by him, even though temporarily it might be held back for independent use in industry.

The Expenditure of the Surplus.

Of this 40 per cent., some 10 per cent. might be invested as savings for capital extension by the Industrial Trusts; 15 per cent. might be taxed by the State or municipality for communal expenditure; and the remaining 15 per cent. would be available for use by the Social Service Trusts.

The 15 per cent. expended by the State and municipalities would presumably be applied in much the same manner as at present, though items might change in amount, insignificant sums being spent on " law and order "; great increases on education and housing; and large subsidies being made for the improve-

ment of transport, land values, and other public
utilities.

The 15 per cent. spent by the Social Service Trusts
(including the Central Trust) would be applied for all
social items for which individual bent and initiative
are required, or which can be most effectively administered by relatively small bodies : research; educational experiment; constructive art; opera; travelling fellowships; communal buildings; local housing
schemes; grants to those who showed ingenuity in
domestic architecture; and a wide range of club and
evening activities.

Such a scheme of distribution would have the
essential virtue of building from the base upwards.
A foundation would be made by raising all persons
to the average wage, and by perfect hygiene and
housing. Then the distribution of means for expression above that level would be according to genius.
The spendthrifts, acknowledged and urged on by
others, would be men skilled in discovery and art.

Unemployment.

Extravagance in spending is sometimes justified
on the ground that it gives work; and, conversely,
self-limitation is condemned because it is believed to
cause loss of work. This is, of course, absurd. If a
person refrains from building a mansion in order to
found a college, the net effect on employment is nil.

In general, whenever individuals restrict their personal expenditure and use the funds instead for social ends, the result is to divert, but not to destroy, employment.

In the theoretical régime outlined here unemployment could be almost entirely avoided. In the first place, there would be immense industrial and social enterprises under the control of bodies nationally co-ordinated. Most of these enterprises would be capable of extension or contraction at will, and might be used to balance fluctuations in unco-ordinated industry. Whenever there occurred a slump in the activity of unco-ordinated trade, national schemes of expenditure would be increased; a smooth average level of trade would thus be preserved.

Such national enterprise could not be extended indefinitely, however, if it were unprofitable. . It might be subsidised by the raiding of funds destined for other purposes, but that would, again, only divert, and not increase employment. Thus, in addition to extensive national works a further element is required in any scheme for the continuous avoidance of unemployment—namely, some means of making the works profitable. This could be provided either through controlling the supply of money and the general level of prices, or through the adjustment of wage costs.

Wages, to consider the second alternative, might be fixed by some National Wages Board, acting upon

two main criteria : the principle of fixing individual
wages according to skill; and the principle of maintaining an average, or general, level of wages such
that industry might at all times profitably expand.
The average would need to be not so low as to cause
a falling off in the demand for consumers' goods, and
not so high as to raise costs unduly in proportion to
prices. In this attempt they would manifestly have
the goodwill of all parties; for since the whole of
the community would sink or swim together, all
would be anxious that the general level of wages
should be adjusted to whatever position would lead
to the greatest activity in industry, and to the lowest
degree of unemployment.

Industrial Relations.

The generalisation of the Society's principles relating to property and ownership would produce a situation in which almost all persons would have the
double function of employer and employee. Since
all would begin their working career without inherited
capital, they would at least have to start in the
ranks, as employees. The few who arrived rapidly
at positions of management, and were able to save
enough to establish independent businesses, could, if
they wished, thereby avoid the rôle of employee.
The remainder, however, would throughout be the
employees of the Industrial Trusts.

As members of such Trusts they would also be
P

employers. Since each Trust would own industrial
shares, any member of it would be a trustee shareholder; and through his membership he could exercise
the powers of a shareholder.

In addition, every employee would become an
employer through the generalising of a further
principle. The firms held by the Trusts would be
owned on the basis of co-partnership, the employees
in each firm being given, as a group, a proportion
of shares carrying rights of control. *Qua* employee,
every person would thus be partner in the particular
unit in which he was engaged.

The situation thus visualised is one in which an
employer would be indistinguishable from an employee
—and in which no "industrial relations" as now
understood could exist, since there would not be two
separate parties to be related to one another. Industry would be composed of a vast number of teams,
each member of a team having a double rôle.

Taxation and Government Expenditure.

A further question which has a theoretical setting,
but also a certain practical implication, is : If all
men were contributive, would there be need for law
and government ? In other words, if all were bent
on service, and upon serving the same ends, would
it not be impossible for their interests to conflict;
and if there were no conflict, would not government
and law be superfluous ? All economic and social

life might surely then be, with perfect safety, anarchistic.

The response to this appears to be that, in the first place, although men may be agreed upon broad philosophic aims, they may find disagreement both as to the particular practical aims and as to the method of achieving them. Wide scope for discord may be found among those who profess identical beliefs. Secondly, the economic contributive life is only one part of the totality of life; thus, although relative smoothness might be secured within business through the joining of all efforts, this would yield no guarantee that there would be concord in other spheres. Offence may be given through casual driving, promiscuity, breach of promise, neglect, or inconsiderateness; and wherever waywardness of any kind means hurt to others, there must be some recognised procedure for treating the case and some criteria for bringing it to an issue. The general body of such criteria is the law. And all such law must presumably be arrived at by democratic process— one man, one vote.

Hence, irrespective of the stage of growth reached in economic matters, there will still be a necessity for State organisation, law, and government, of much the same kind as that which exists now, so long as any form of disregard or carelessness prevails. Wherever self-interests clash, law is needed to establish the line dividing and defending them.

It follows, therefore, that the Contributive Society's organisation could never completely supplant that of the State. The Society would deal purely with the administration of certain economic and social affairs; and the State would still remain supreme, determining not only the liberties and rights of subjects within the personal and family sphere, but to some extent also the activity of the Society itself and of its various Trusts.

A typical example of the relation between the State and the Society may be shown by the consideration of taxation. The State, through Parliament, would need to secure most of its revenue from the regular receipts of the Society, which it would tax for this purpose. The problem would perpetually arise : How much of the Society's surplus (about 30 per cent, of the total National Income, excluding savings) should be absorbed by the State, and how much should be left for expenditure by the Society? The point of principle to be considered is this : in the case of all money spent by the State the method of expenditure would be purely communal; that is, it would be spent by committees or administrators appointed and controlled by or on behalf of the whole body of the people. In the case of the money spent by the Society, the method of expenditure would be mainly individual. Members making donations to the Society would separately determine upon which social services their own donations would be spent; and much individual initiative would remain in the choice of the objects of expenditure. The issue is, then : How much of the total national surplus should be spent communally, and how much individually ? It seems clear that a combination of the two methods of spending is the ideal : not all expenditure should be purely communal; and not all should be purely individual. Communal spending often yields the highest value; but it leaves the decision as to which things, in fact, are of value, to committees or to a majority vote. The choice may be unduly plebeian, and may prevent the rarer, unconventional desires of the community from finding expression. Some decentralised control of spending seems necessary if progress is to be made in the evolution of taste and variety and in the emergence of new values.

The need for deciding the proportionate division of funds between communal and individual expenditure will arise much before ideal society is reached : indeed, in a minor way the problem exists now in the case of charitable and insurance funds. It arises, for instance, in the discussion of " family endowment." But the subject is introduced here, in the consideration of the ideal state, mainly with a view to suggesting that, at all stages of social evolution, a distinction will probably be desirable between the State proper and the personal economic organisation of the community.

In the situation which would emerge through the

generalising of the Society's principles there would still remain the political machine as an entity distinct and dominant. And there would still remain a problem of taxation. The Parliament, democratically appointed as at present, would impose taxes either directly on the Society or indirectly on commodities. But there would be a limit to the amount of taxation it would be desirable to impose, even though all persons were contributive. If, for instance, the direct tax laid on the Society were to absorb all its surplus available for social use, there could be no individual spending for social purposes. This would diminish somewhat the incentive to produce. For whereas a person may be violently enthusiastic as a producer if he is allowed to spend the income derived upon objects which to him, personally, seem significant, he may be less ready to pour funds into the lap of a State Department or a Committee whose policies he doubts. To gain the highest net result a due balance is thus needed between the amount of revenue drawn by the State for communal outlay, and the amount left in the hands of the Trusts or other organs of the Society for decentralised and more individual spending.

Equality.

Æsthetically, equality is a thing to loathe. It means, in metaphor, land with no hills, a sea planed of its waves, or a race deprived of human peaks. A régime which ruled all to a common average would strike much from life, both in its physical and spiritual expression, first limiting possessions, then, through them indirectly, limiting people. For it would begin by causing all to frame their physical life to a confined pattern; to build their homes much to pattern; to dress, furnish, take their pleasures, and make their meals to pattern. Then, conformity in deeds would inevitably bring in its train conformity in spirit. When the non-conforming mind is deprived of an outlet, it must in the course of time lose strength. Conventions emerge and check spontaneity, each individual being held and circumscribed and trimmed by his social circle. Society stiffens : and sinks, if averaging is the rule, to a dull level of mediocrity.

It is a sombre paradox that the days when truly big things were done, and done in the name of Art, were when equality was not conceived. Slaves built the Pyramids. Slaves and sweated labour built the best temples and cathedrals. Now we have no comparable power to create these things; we are made impotent by the strength of our fellow feelings.

There is a certain inevitability in this. A small sacrifice made universally by the multitude who form the basis of society renders possible, here and there, building to enormous heights. Conversely, an enormous sacrifice from the heights is needed to make a slight universal improvement at the base. This would suggest, then, a reason for our present inability, despite an immense increase in resources, to touch the earlier levels of art. The more humanitarian we become, the more, other things being equal, do we sap resources from above in order to give strength beneath; by the very power of social feeling we thus, as a community, flatten our performance and ambition. Such a levelling process would be carried to its extreme by any system founded without reservation on equality or " averaging." Unmodified equality would imply not only courting sameness throughout society, but with set purpose excluding all else. It would mean the annihilation, unrelieved, of all things personal which require an outlay exceeding the average, and would bring society and every physically established feature of society to a single fixed stratum.

It is impossible to feel that such a condition is the ideal. It might be immeasurably better than the present state, with its squalid depths. But it cannot be the ideal. There must result a sense of stifling, a suffocation, if it is known that in every personal walk of life a rigid physical limit is set to expression. In the present state there is no certainty in the limit for a wide group of the community; and there is no prohibition for anyone from striving against the limit. Under unconditional equality there can, however, be neither the power nor the hope of attaining higher expression; and it is impossible for any one person to aid others to improvement except through some infinitesimal increase in the average.

Indeed it would seem that, once the base of the

social structure had been made sound, a society bent
on contribution would collect itself for an intense
effort to escape from deadening monotony. It would
concentrate on building upwards, in spires, from the
solid base. In such an attempt there would be two
main forms of building : that which implies corporate
expression; and that which implies individual expression. In both cases variety, and grandeur, and scope
would seem indispensable to achievement.

The chief forms of corporate expression which en-
hance life are civic architecture and town-planning,
memorials, cathedrals, national art and opera, and
parks and green spaces and the care of natural scenes.
Perhaps the supreme height of achievement in this
sphere is the Vienna " Ring." For one cannot escape
the feeling there that, whatever may be the personal
standard of living of the Viennese, they must gain
exhilaration and spiritual quality merely from contact with their greater communal radiance. Subconsciously, if not consciously, there must be drawn
from this daily scene something which helps to sustain
that most sensitive exuberance of the people.

It is evident that any society founded on the
general pooling of surplus will have a high power of
corporate expression; and in this particular respect
the Society considered here would be unusually
strong. The 30 per cent. of the National Income
available for social spending represents a sum comparable with about half that annually squandered

during the War. With such an amount slums would be swept away in the first few years and a programme of constructive building might be pursued such that in minimum time every town would be a gallery of parks and palaces. We could again build Pyramids, no longer through the power of slavery, but of a communal symbolism.

But corporate expression is not in itself sufficient. There must be individual expression. For instance, externally it might be possible to preserve the country house, and vicarage, and castle by converting them into "institutions" and owning them communally. But they would not be the same. Something utterly irreplaceable would be lost unless the occupants by birth, the persons who have grown up with them and learnt their atmosphere, remain in ownership. They are not "things" in the sense of being dead, but the living expression of those who made and tended them. And if they are to continue living and retain their spirit, they must retain also those who have dwelt in them. This implies inequality of personal spending.

What is true of these traits in the personality of the countryside is true in less degree of all self-expression through ownership. Whatever completes or gives appropriate "clothing" to a personality, whether it be actual clothing, or a house and garden, or a horse, or other animal friend, is a contribution to variety and art. It is a unit in communal life and, to that extent, a gift to the community.

That this kind of individual personality expression must be preserved seems almost axiomatic. And a society bent on averaging would, it seems, have to allow latitude for it, or be condemned.

In the Society we are considering the latitude would have to come from personal judgment; for, from the beginning, it is here assumed that every act is voluntary. It is true that the Society as a body might prompt individual expression of this kind in various ways, say, by grants to persons who showed genius, or by displays of home architecture; but the chief decision would remain with the individual. Each would independently decide whether he could add to the communal pageantry most by expenditure below, at, or above the average wage.

Can anything precise survive such a discussion in which the only principle is compromise and in which every person compromises differently? It is indeed difficult to see clear light; and, at best, only a general line of guidance can be distinguished. Briefly it would be this. Social feeling and humanitarianism seem to be the primary, indispensable basis of society, since without them society would have no meaning. These, then, would demand *as a first step* anxiety to destroy sordidness and squalor and attend to those whose need is greatest. Until this step had been taken and a situation reached in which all men had some reasonably full power of self-expression, it would seem that only in exceptional cases would men feel that their maximum contribution was being made if they lived substantially above the average. There would undoubtedly be exceptions : for instance, persons in public office or whose place in life is that of professional host, and persons who are the obvious guardians of some unique homestead. But the exceptions would probably not be a high percentage ; and voluntary equality in personal spending would tend to become the rule.

At a later stage, assuming that a large majority of the community were contributive and that the social basis had been made sound, the *relative* value of variety would be placed higher, and in the complex of communal art each person would tend towards the belief that he could contribute most by being most fully himself. Whoever possessed the gift of personal expression through things would surround himself with the things that harmonised ; and he who felt the need of mountains or of the sea to live ecstatically would seek their company, knowing that the cost was justified by the higher life-art reached.

In essence, the thought here is that, although equality must rank high as an initial aim, being the inevitable outcome of that sympathy which gives society its meaning, yet there is beyond and above and almost absorbing it a further aim, which we may call the Higher Beauty. By this is meant the art expression of the whole body of the people, viewed as a harmony : a thing of infinite variety combined into one vast life symphony. It is the counterpart in man's activity of that of Nature, where infinitesimals and infinites contrast, and where nothing is so small as to be neglected and nothing so great as to overbear the whole. It is this human Higher Beauty that demands the contribution of each artist; and it is this in the service of which each may acquire freedom, partly because its service means full outreaching, partly because it implies unison and not conflict with other effort.

INDEX

*Where the reference is to a theme covering a sequence of pages, the
number of the first page only is given.*

222

"THE NEIGHBOURS, LIMITED"

BY

J. R. BELLERBY

Fellow of Gonville and Caius College, Cambridge

A paper read before the Political Economy Club, Cambridge, by request of the Chairman, J. M. Keynes, 6 May 1929

THE study of the "ideal state" is one which seems to deserve more attention than is customarily given to it. In the past there has been a tendency to assume that a subject so remote from current reality is suitable for treatment only by visionaries or romanticists; and professional economists have for the most part avoided it. Such an attitude is not perhaps readily explained; for the study of the ideal state stands in the same direct relation to the rest of economics as, for instance, the study of architecture does to building. The theory of the ideal state is the theory of "purposive" construction, of the final aim and art of social development. It is clearly an indispensable part of the science of economics; and it is peculiarly practical; for, without some vision of the ultimate economic structure, all current building may be on wrong foundations or ill-balanced, and in the long run may yield no substantial progress.

Moreover, it is the subject of most vivid interest to those outside economics. Their concern is almost always to discover how things may be improved; to learn whether their vision of better things can be realised; and they would gain most if by any means they could secure some view of the finally desired régime as a coherent and comprehensive picture.

For instance, the essential interest of any civil or public body, whether of the city or the State, is to learn what is the ideal relationship to be achieved between industry and Government. To what extent should the State intervene in the organisation of business and in quickening its growth? In the final stage, would there be a necessity for the Government to intervene at all? In fact, would there be any need for government?

The philosopher has another problem. Life holds certain values, some having a physical basis, others spiritual. There is an evident relation between the two. The physical aspects of life may be expanded to the detriment of the spiritual, and *vice versa*. There is good for the body and good for the soul. Sometimes the one supports the other and sometimes it does not. The power to achieve the exact harmony of the two depends mainly, however, on the way in which industry is organised, that is, on the nature of the system. What, then, is the "ideal" system, the system which will yield both types of values in the highest degree?

Still another question may come from the pulpit. Is any organisation of industry possible which will enable every individual in it to apply in and through his trade the principles of an accepted religious creed? Must industry inevitably be a sphere outside religion; or is there not some way of organising it so that business itself may be an expression of belief? The concern, again, is not so much with what exists as with what might be. A pointer is desired to something "beyond."

Then there is the dweller-in-the-slum. Inevitably he sees industry through darkened glasses. His vision of it is coloured only by the waste-heaps. The one thought is: "Nothing can be worse; what can be found that is better?" And the only answer for him, at present, comes from Marx.

What is everyone's affair is, of course, nobody's affair—and this may perhaps account for the dearth of economic writing on the ideal state in the last century. The point of concern, however, is that there still exists the gap; and that there is still an emphatic demand for the means of filling it. The problem of the final aim of economic effort enters virtually every other social problem; and for that reason it lies subconsciously if not actively, in the minds of all. If economists could give the lead, by establishing a reasoned body of opinion on the nature of the ideal system, the outside world would ask little more of them.

SOME FEATURES OF THE IDEAL SYSTEM

Two methods might be suggested for discovering the main characteristics of the ultimate desired state. One would be to begin by considering what are the "fundamental values" in life, the human ends to be served, and then discuss the form of economic system most capable of securing those ends. In other words, the ideal economic system may be defined as "that form of economic organisation which would most effectively lead to the achievement of human purpose." The economic system is only a means to other ends. And if these other "ends" are capable of being clearly shown, then the ideal system can be no other than that which leads to them most rapidly.

Another method of discovering the nature of the ideal system is through the consideration of the individual in it. If it is desired to know, for instance, what a Christian society would be like, all that is necessary is to assume that the individual members of society are themselves Christian, and then consider how they must act. Similarly, the nature of the "ideal" system can be found by assuming the existence of a body of "ideal" economic men, carefully defined, and then determining how they would act. The economic system, in essence, is nothing but the established conduct, or business habits, of those who work within it. Ideal persons will establish ideal habits; and their system will be perfect.

The definition of the ideal system, under this second method of approach, is therefore "that form of economic organisation which would *emerge* if all individuals in it were of desired quality."

Whichever beginning is used, it is inevitable that the start must be made from dogma. If the ideal society is defined as that which most fully serves human ends, then it is necessary to state dogmatically what these ends are. Similarly if the ideal society is regarded as that which would emerge, given individuals of the desired stuff, it is necessary to state a belief as to the stuff in reality most desired. The fact that the start is made from dogma does not, however, destroy the argument. All reasoning proceeds from assumption, hypothesis, faith. To begin with dogma is merely to begin with the inevitable.

It is proposed here to approach the nature of the ideal system from the consideration of the individual, a description being given at the outset of the type of "economic man" to be assumed. (The other definition of ideal society will be applied at the end essentially as a test.)

Thus, the dogma from which the start is to be made is that *the ideal system will emerge when all individuals in it are bent on contributing their maximum to the well-being of society as a whole.* More precisely, the individual of our imagining is he who is anxious to maximise his *net* gift to society: the net gift being the amount he produces and puts into the communal pool *less* the amount he takes out of the pool and consumes. His concern is with the difference, or margin, between what he produces and what he consumes.

The motive assumed here is seen to be the reverse of that generally imputed to the "economic man" of the present time. Whereas this abstract representative of human kind is usually regarded as being bent on maximum acquisition, he is assumed here to have the aim of maximum contribution.

If this definition of the ideal "economic man" is acceptable, there remain no serious difficulties in deriving the nature of the ideal system. The rest follows as a matter of logic, without further assumptions. The principal features of the ideal system, and much of the detail, can be discovered by the simple process of assuming the existence of, say, twenty such "economic men," and considering how they would act.

It will be necessary, in order to carry out this process, to imagine the group of twenty in different situations and confronting different problems of economic principle: problems of consumption and distribution; of property and inheritance; and of competition and business organisation; the aim being to discover how the group, having their stated motive, would react to each problem.

PERSONAL CONSUMPTION

The first and perhaps the most intractable question before the group would be that of deciding at what level to fix the personal consumption of the members. It has been noted that when anyone desires to maximise his *net* gift to society, there are two points to which he must attend: the increase of the amount he produces, and the decrease of the amount he consumes. The first part, that of increasing service to the rest of society, is relatively simple; it merely involves the conversion of the individual into a voluntary sweated labourer, producing all he can.

The task of cutting down personal consumption is not so easy. The difficulty from the theoretical point of view is to decide at what stage the cutting down of consumption may lead to loss of efficiency and thus to a reduced *net* contribution to society. Efficiency frequently depends on things essentially atmospheric, or psychic. Sometimes it depends on the ability to escape into a corner, away from the obtrusions of fellow men; sometimes on the ability to see green things and to feel at peace with the world. In all cases the effect on efficiency of reducing personal consumption must be extremely difficult to gauge; and it must vary widely for different persons.

Then there are other problems. Much of a person's production, if this term includes all forms of service to others, is not measurable. Unpaid social services, for instance, do not lend themselves to measurement. Thus, if anyone cuts down his personal consumption, at the expense of that part of his production which is not measurable, he is unable to decide whether he has increased or decreased his *net* contribution. For example, if one of our group of twenty were to walk some miles during the day to avoid consuming transport services, the time lost might diminish his power of service through, say, the organising of a boys' club, or the writing of voluntary articles. He will have cut down his "consumption" of transport services by a measurable amount. But his "production" has been reduced by an unknown amount; and he is therefore unable to say whether there has been a gain or loss in his *net* contribution.

Instances of this kind might be multiplied to show that the adjusting of personal consumption to efficiency level presents many problems, and is in all cases a highly individual matter. The solution for no two persons will be exactly alike. And if it is difficult for any single individual to reach a decision for himself, it must be many times more difficult for a group or a society to lay down a rule for all.

Granted, however, all the difficulties, there would seem no escape for the group from the necessity of laying down some fairly definite principle of personal consumption. If there is one sphere in which the members would desire most to have some clear line of action it would be in this sphere of personal conduct. Vagueness on this point would mean that there could be no acid test whereby a member could determine whether he was in fact a contributive person.

Some principle would therefore be needed, which, whilst leaving a certain amount of latitude to the individuals concerned, would be capable of including them all. In other words, the principle would define some level of personal expenditure as a maximum.

On what basis, then, would the maximum be fixed? For this the group might derive some inspiration from another part of the basic definition. The "economic man" has been defined as he who is desirous of serving Society *as a whole*. In other words, the entire community is taken as the family unit; and all members are pooling surplus for that wider unit. This adds, then, a new thought: the notion of sharing or averaging of benefits. There is a quality of politeness ordinarily exercised around the family table, which prevents each member from grasping everything in reach, and leads him to attend to his neighbours first, and not take more than his share. The same politeness, we may assume, would be extended to include the whole of Society, and would lead to a tendency to share, or average out, the things produced.

One feels that Bernard Shaw is fundamentally sound in regarding the average wage as the core of Socialism. Clearly, a society that does not share is no society at all. And it is almost certain that the group of twenty, with their wider view of social relations, would select the average wage as maximum, and adopt that as their principle of consumption. This seems to follow from the definition.

In parenthesis, it might be suggested that Shaw is probably not equally sound in believing that it is possible to *impose* equality on all people. No dictatorship, either of an individual or of a majority of acquisitors, could accomplish this. Moreover, there seems some question whether, in the *ultimate* ideal, there will be equality in all things. Equality means, almost inevitably, uniformity. And uniformity leads to convention, flatness, a dull level of mediocrity. There is a distressing amount of this in the present, and one shrinks from the idea of still more in prospect. What seems probable is that, in the ideal, there will be much more communal magnificence; there will be a return to the building of pyramids, by voluntary process. As regards personal spending, there will be inequalities, but any departure from uniformity will be at the request of the majority. In other words, some members of society will live in large houses, and have personal expenditure in excess of that of others; but they themselves will only tolerate this state of affairs because they have been requested by the rest of society to do it, to add more variety and light and shade to life. They would be the persons selected, on grounds of special sensitiveness, to hold the position of public host or hostess, or guardian of the countryside.

To return to the group of twenty, there seems little question that, acting in the present, each member individually would attempt to reach the "politeness" level, and would not be disposed to depart from that level, once attained, unless particularly requested to do so by the remaining members of the group.

From this, one principle may be derived, as being probably a basic feature of the ideal system: the voluntary self-imposition of the average wage, departure from this level being only at the insistence of other citizens.

If it may be assumed that each member has solved his personal problem and has reached a position to contribute, he will then meet the wider problem: Towards what ends is the contribution to be made? One of the earliest tasks of the group of twenty would be to define carefully its aims. If it failed in this it would fall into the same predicament as the uplift association which had for its motto, "We build," but found no answer to give when asked what it was that they built.

The task of defining aims would not be as easy as might at first appear, for since the contribution of each individual would mean the giving of virtually his entire substance, the object of the giving would need to be of unquestioned weight. Moreover, it would be essential to preserve full consistency in the aims; otherwise the pursuit of one might clash with the attainment of the another. This means, then, that the aims would have to be derived from some conscious and concerted philosophy; and the starting-point of the group, in any discussion of objectives, would need to be a statement of their belief as to "fundamental values."

Briefly, and very inadequately, some thoughts may be offered here as to the manner in which a scheme of ultimate values might be framed. First, there are two spheres in which values having an essentially physical basis are to be found. One is the sphere of art and beauty, poetry and music; in a word, that of the pursuit of the aesthetic. Within this field of things to be sought after is to be included not only the creation of those positive harmonies which are spoken of as art, but also the destruction of disharmonies: noise, dirt, and ugliness. Such aims can be widely achieved only on the basis of immense economic effort, and the "values" drawn from them of beauty or aesthetic quality arise definitely from physical striving.

The second sphere in which similar "values" may arise is that of discovery, the pursuit of the unknown. Again this field of aims embraces both the search for things desired, and the pruning away of things undesired. There is the removal of ignorance and stupidity on the one hand, and, on the other, the growth of understanding, reason, range of vision, knowledge. In this case also the creation of the values involves a foundation of immense physical activity.

Then, assuming that these two types of physical strife, the search for beauty and the search for knowledge, are themselves worthwhile, it is possible to draw from them a by-product which is perhaps itself the summit of all value—personality. In seeking the physical worth-while ends men may develop certain spiritual qualities—those pertaining to character—stubbornness, patience, a sense of humour, and social feeling. These form a third and final group of essential aims.

These three groups are curiously interwoven. If art and music are taken away, the values which remain seem arid. Wisdom, and even virtue, have a sense of starkness unless lightened by some form of art. Then, if wisdom is removed, it means that everything in life springs surely from untutored feeling or blind instinct. It means a muddle-headed virtue, if that is possible.

Finally, the spiritual values are themselves incapable of being formed except on the basis of physical activity. One cannot gain courage or determination unless there is something about which to be determined. To love the community means nothing unless there is something to do for the community. It is in the doing, and pursuing, and resisting of *things* that the by-product of character may emerge.

Thus, each of the three groups of values depends for much of its merit, and even for its existence, on the co-existence of the other groups. There is a richness and a greater harmony and fulness in the joining of the three.

Such, then, in scanty outline, is the trend along which a theory of values might be evolved.

Given any such philosophy, the group of twenty whose problems are being reviewed would find themselves under the necessity of expressing it in terms of current practical action. This would present little difficulty; a list could readily be drawn up, comprehensive enough to cover every type of activity which would lead to the attainment of the triple purpose. Under "The Search for Beauty" might be comprised: the promotion of art, the preservation of urban and rural beauty, the destruction of dirt, noise, and disease, and the clearing of open spaces. Under "The Search for Knowledge" would be included: the development of educational principle, the setting up of schools, the provision of funds for research, and the establishing of libraries and good laboratories. Under "Personality and Goodwill" would come all work of welfare: the setting up of boys' and girls' clubs, the provision of holiday camps, prison reform, professional almoning, the giving of legal advice to the poor, the care of the aged, and the wider tasks of promoting industrial and international peace.

A list of this nature would be necessary to the members of the group in order to show, in concrete expression, what were the aims they had in common. Thereafter, the problem confronting them would simply be how best to organise themselves for a combined advance on these aims.

THE DISPOSAL OF PROPERTY

The situation reached by the group of twenty, after the two main problems so far discussed had been settled, would be this. Each member, having cut down his personal expenses to efficiency level, would have a surplus of income, and possibly some capital, to contribute. Further, each member, having found himself able to subscribe to the philosophy of the society as expressed in its social aims, would know precisely towards what ends his surplus was to be contributed. The task remaining would therefore be to decide what method would be most efficient for administering, controlling, and holding the surplus capital and income of the members, and applying it to the social aims. Would better results be gained from individual control and ownership, or would some method of pooling the surplus, so as to yield a form of corporate ownership, prove better? What seems probable is that, to secure the best results, some form of compromise between these two would be needed. That is, not all the surplus income and capital would be controlled individually, and not all of it would be pooled. And even in the case of that part which was pooled, some measure of individual discretion as to its subsequent disposal would be preserved.

In any compromise of this nature the decision reached as to the actual proportion of capital and income to be retained in private hands must depend to some extent on personal preference. It would seem impossible to arrive at one rule for all, and any attempt to achieve precise uniformity would be destined almost certainly to destroy the experiment itself.

One possible way of indicating how a suitable compromise between private ownership and corporate ownership might be reached would be to explain what is about to be attempted by a circle of seven or eight persons in the near future. "The Neighbours" aim, briefly, is to discover the correct way of applying the contributive principle to the problem of ownership of property, and the decision which has been reached is broadly along these lines.

INCOME

As regards the current income received by a person from his work or investments, little difficulty is met. Suppose that the person is receiving £500 gross income per year. Of this he will need to retain, say, £150 a year for personal expenditure. In addition, he may need £50 for the support of local charities, his church, and his political party. These amounts will be spent directly by himself. The sum of £300 is then left over for the promotion of objects selected in agreement with his fellows.

This £300 it is proposed, should be pooled with the surplus income of the others of the group. To make this possible the members will form themselves into a friendly society, legally established and empowered to receive and administer the donations of the members. Thus, the £300 will be handed over as a gift to the society, which will then invest it and use the interest year by year for the promotion of the selected aims.

It is proposed that each member shall reserve full discretion as to the proportion of his income which is to be retained and spent by him privately. Further, it is intended that, as regards that portion which is handed over to the society, the donor shall retain the right to decide in what direction the interest from it shall be spent, i.e. whether it shall be devoted to some scheme of education, or to slum clearance, or to any other selected social aim.

In this way, although the actual legal ownership of the

property is transferred from the individual to the society, the individual preserves his *stewardship* of it. He still controls the manner in which his own earnings are employed.

This policy of preserving individual stewardship seems to be in full accordance with the contributive principle, since the motive to contribute must itself be much strengthened if the individual retains the power to decide the precise manner in which his own contribution is to be made.

Existing Capital

The proposal at present favoured by the members of the projected society in respect of existing capital, i.e. capital already in the possession of a member, is that only a minor portion of it should be handed over to the society until the member has reached mature status.

It would not be desired of a member up to the age of thirty, nor necessarily expected of him up to the age of forty, that he should relinquish to any large extent his private control of capital. This is, however, a matter of present expediency rather than of accepted principle. The real principle held by the society is expressed in its expectation that, by the age of forty, a member shall have placed substantially the whole of his capital in some form of corporate ownership. The capital need not all be handed over to the society itself; it may be used in part for providing insurance or for the purchase of an annuity (though the society will make provision for a member to the extent of his donation to it), or it may be placed in a trust for purposes of education, or for use in religious or political or independent charitable pursuits. In one form or another, however, the capital is to be corporately held when the member has reached the stage in life of being able to realise what his settled aims, aspirations, and responsibilities are likely to be.

It may be noted that whatever happens to the capital, the member concerned will still retain a large degree of stewardship over it, either through defining the terms of the trust in which it is placed, or through controlling the direction in which it is employed by the society.

The specific advantages of corporate ownership over private ownership of capital, from the point of view of the contributive individual, would be that: (*a*) any losses of capital would fall on the whole group, and joint ownership would mean greater security than private ownership; (*b*) the administration of the capital would be in the most expert hands of the group, and would relieve the other individuals entirely for their productive tasks; (*c*) the capital would continue to be applied to social purposes after the member's death and would not be squandered; (*d*) there would be a certain psychological effect upon persons outside the group, and a fashion might result of viewing property more in the light of stewardship than of ownership; (*e*) it would signify a first step towards the abolition of inheritance and would achieve this without destroying savings.

BUSINESS PRINCIPLES

So far, the basic problems of distribution, property, and inheritance have been considered, but there remains still untouched a vast range of questions relating to the way in which the "economic man," as defined, would conduct himself in business. The group of twenty, to return to the original imaginary party, in applying their principle of contribution to everyday industry, would find themselves confronted throughout by innumerable minor problems and, as a preliminary to launching their attack on these, they would first need to decide whether a contributive individual could hope to survive at all in a mainly acquisitive regime.

Since space is limited, it may perhaps be excusable to suggest certain findings without offering full support for them. In general, it seems that a contributive person could survive in competition in the present regime wherever his task was one involving organisation, leadership, foresight, imagination, or hard work. He could probably survive, for example, in those parts of industry which involve extractive or manufacturing processes, or artistic or constructive capacity. In these cases the only person who makes large profits in the long run is he who attracts custom by good quality, secures the co-operation of employees through fair treatment, and reduces costs through the adoption of modern methods.

Much more doubt arises in the case of merchanting and the commercial sphere of business. Wherever profit is made on the narrow margin between the cost and the sale price of a commodity, the trader who benefits most is he who can drive a hard bargain. And although driving hard bargains may be good business, it has little to do with contribution; there is nothing constructive in it. Hence there would seem to be numerous branches of commerce and transport—though this does not apply to all—in which a contributive person would find little play for his talents, and little prospect of surviving in the stream of competition.

This does not mean that there is no way of handling the commercial part of industry to render it wholly contributive; it means only that the task may be beyond the power of single individuals acting in the present. The purchase and sale of commodities at wholesale is an indispensable part of industry, and is, therefore, constructive in its net effects, and it could be rendered completely constructive, without waste of any kind, if the system of competitive merchanting were replaced by co-operative buying and selling. That would be, as it were, the "contributive" way. But it would not be within the power of action of a group of twenty, and in all probability the members of the group now under discussion would be disposed to shun those branches of commerce which seemed to handicap the non-acquisitive person.

It would be fascinating and not unfruitful to apply the contributive principle to every problem of trade, and discover what type of action would be dictated by it. How, on this basis, for instance, would an employer act with regard to the use of patents and the preservation of trade secrets, the determination of wages and of other conditions of labour, and the control of policy and management? There is no limit to problems of this kind. All that one would wish to say, however, is that there is a solution in each case, and that the application of the solution would not mean destruction to the firm applying it. That is, the contributive principle is capable of application at once by single individuals over a large part of industry, and ultimately over the whole of industry, when a sufficient number of persons have been converted from the acquisitive to the contributive intent.

When that stage is reached we shall begin to approach the ideal. If the broad lines of the reasoning here are acceptable, the principal features of the ideal state are shown to be: (1) the voluntary restraint of personal consumption to about the average; (2) the voluntary pooling of surplus income and capital for social purposes; (3) the voluntary surrender of inheritance rights; (4) an attempt on the part of each individual in industry to apply the principle of maximum net contribution in all situations.

In the ideal state there will be as much independence and personal initiative as now, enterprise will still be privately conducted, but for public gain, and each individual will retain stewardship over whatever wealth he personally can create. There will be as much variety then as now and, in some ways, more, since communal outlay will be more lavish. Individual freedom will reach its full limit, a condition possible only when each member of society desires those things which do not involve his trespassing on the preserves of others. When all have a similar goal, their efforts harmonise, each attains full freedom, and gives and takes his quota of goodwill.

At the beginning, two definitions were given of the ideal state, the one being used to aid the discovery of its main principles, the other to be applied at the end as a test. Under the second definition, the ideal state was to be regarded as that which "would most effectively lead to the achievement of human purpose." The only system which can meet this test is one in which all members have satisfied themselves as to the essential purpose of their existence, and, having done this, are prepared to co-operate with others of similar mind. In other words, it must be some system in which the members have formed a settled judgment as to human "ends," and have then joined forces in the attempt to build an organisation specifically designed for the attainment of these ends.

ECONOMICS, WELFARE AND BELLERBY'S *CONTRIBUTIVE SOCIETY*

BY

ALAN HARRISON

Reader in Agricultural Economics,
University of Reading

Hirsch and the Social Limits to Growth

The arguments assembled by Fred Hirsch in his book, *Social Limits to Growth* (1977), have received wide acclaim on account of the penetrating and novel insights they provide into the nature of economic development and the problems that come in its wake. His analysis has been and continues to be widely publicised. Although his conclusions have not gone unchallenged in every detail, nevertheless they remain largely unscathed in spite of the detailed examination to which they have been subjected and are remarkable for the degree of novelty with which they continue to be regarded. Yet, it will be argued here, not only were a number of Hirsch's central ideas the concern of J. R. Bellerby in his book, *A Contributive Society*, published forty-six years earlier than *Social Limits to Growth*, but Hirsch's more radical conclusions were not only anticipated by Bellerby but developed and refined by him to a degree which Hirsch failed to achieve.

The main lines of Hirsch's work can be summarised for present purposes as follows: the more developed, prosperous and commercialised societies become, the more consumption and living patterns take on social attributes. It is not simply that as demand grows it generates greater competition for resources—though that does happen—but (p. 3) "conditions of use tend to deteriorate as use becomes more widespread", that is (p. 4), "satisfaction of . . . individual preferences itself alters the situation that faces others seeking to satisfy similar wants". The whole complex array of goods, services, work positions and social relationships alters as development takes place in ways which he conveniently labelled "positional"; they become, that is, less and less a question of intrinsic merit and more and more one of relationship to other goods, to other users and to setting of use. Competition for place grows relative to competition for performance, which results in added "deadweight" costs for all—social waste.

Such waste is further compounded as modern society becomes more mobile socially as well as geographically. The outcomes of individual behaviour become (p. 88) more "diffused and uncertain in their incidence"; the result is it becomes increasingly less satisfactory to rely on self-interest as the driving force to secure the best outcomes for society in the round. It becomes easier and therefore more likely that citizens will take up roles of free-riders, enjoying the fruits of sacrifices of others while contributing nothing themselves. There will be (p. 89) "erosion of conventions about mutual obligation" so that (p. 130) "citizens are discouraged from recognising any obligation not compensated by direct reward (and) the rest of society bears the cost".

The less "advanced" societies are, the more likely their members are to feel (p. 78) "obligations to act in certain mutually supportive ways"; in other words, in simple closely-knit societies where rotation of giving and receiving is frequent, exchange comes close to being a purely private good.

Nevertheless, friendship is more than a private economic good and (p. 80) "the huge increase in personal mobility in modern economies adds to the problem by making sociability more of a public and less of a private good". As Hirsch rather strikingly puts it (p. 79), "The Good Samaritan remedies a market failure". Unhappily (p. 81), "human contact in advanced economies is increasingly sought but decreasingly attained".

As economic growth proceeds and its benefits accrue in the main, and especially in its early stages, to the already privileged and educated, so education comes to be seen as the passport to sharing in those benefits. However, as education is regarded and presented increasingly in vocational terms, so it expands more than do the jobs requiring the educational credentials which it bestows. The costs of screening out the surplus candidates rise as two sets of social costs ensue, those of the screening process itself and those represented by the disappointed expectations of the unsuccessful candidates themselves.

Finally, as economic growth and development take place and life comes to be acted out and evaluated more and more in the market place, so it becomes increasingly likely that the one by one contributions to this process of commercialisation will, in the end, produce outcomes in the aggregate that those members of society, had they been able to make their wishes known, would not have wished to see happen. As Hirsch puts it (p. 18), "choice in the small does not provide choice in the large", and (p. 92) a "tip-over of activities from social to market provision is a neglected example of social irrationality that can result from rational individual economic behaviour".

There is much more in similar vein which there is not space to summarise here. However, Hirsch is not content simply to identify the problems, he also goes some way towards indicating where he thinks the solutions to them lie. Two brief quotations will serve to illustrate the main lines of his thinking on practical policy issues. First, and this is not in the least novel, there is the need to develop ways of internalising social costs, (p. 17), "If both consumer preferences and full social costs could be correctly passed on to producers, fulfillment of (the) preferences of individual consumers would be the accepted goal of the system". Second, and this goes well beyond the cautious pronouncement so typical of positivist economists (p. 10), "The only way of avoiding the competition in frustration is for the people concerned to co-ordinate their objectives in some explicit way, departing from the principle of isolated individual striving". But this is not likely to prove some trivial cosmetic exercise. On the contrary, nothing short of complete economic restructuring of society is likely to serve (p. 118), "the heart of the problem is how the collectivist forces are to be tamed. It remains unclear whether economic and financial stability can be restored short of the fundamental step of validating the distributional outcome by some ethical criterion, striking at the roots of an individualist market economy".

Policies to "soften" market forces have long exercised man's ingenuity as have measures to ensure that private market choices reflect social benefits and costs. Moreover, as Hirsch points out, certain socialised norms of behaviour which determine conventional standards of commercial and business trust and honesty are necessary, otherwise market processes will not operate at all. But, Hirsch is at pains to stress, the problems which beset society in the developed world and which are the major concern of *Social Limits to Growth* cannot be solved through piece-meal adjustment of the rules of the game in the ways that have served in the past (p. 180), "mutual interdependence between the existent social morality and the means of adapting it impedes any speedy resolution of the tensions involved. It also drastically limits what can be expected from technical manipulation alone. Yet economic management in the past generation has relied wholly on such manipulations. The radical aspect of the appropriate solutions for the tensions diagnosed may well be precisely their imprecise, general and evolving form. The prime need is not new instruments but a change in the climate of their use. The radical change needed is to accept that". And later (p. 190), "Solutions that work have traditionally dominated solutions that have ethical appeal. The distinction is now blurred: to work it must be ethically defensible . . . the first necessity is not technical devices but the public acceptance necessary to make them work".

It might have been thought that a conclusion of such dramatic impact and far-reaching implications would have dominated the voluminous debate which has been directed at Hirsch's work. That is not the case; however, it is the aim in this essay to direct attention to just such an "ethically defensible" solution to society's problems based on an analysis similar in many respects to that presented by Hirsch but written almost half a century earlier. It is contained in the book re-issued here: J. R. Bellerby's *A Contributive Society*, first published in 1931. Not only did Bellerby anticipate the *need* for the sort of radical transformation of society that Hirsch envisaged but felt unable to specify in any detail, he set out with clarity, courage, elegance and vigour the ideal form that society should seek to achieve and the practical steps to follow in order to bring about that transformation.

A Contributive Society

Bellerby's arguments are in many respects similar to Hirsch's—surprisingly so given the many years separating the two works. In round terms the case he presents runs as follows: the market system possesses great allocative merits but it is also seriously defective. It does not result in an ethically defensible distribution of income and wealth; in particular, it seriously over-rewards the relatively few who own its capital and under-rewards the many who have only their labour to offer. It imposes heavy costs on the public at large—pollution is the one most frequently quoted, but it is by no means the only one. It encourages much that is unworthy and shoddy. It does not solve satisfactorily the problems that arise when society faces "a limited common fund of goods". It does not provide social capital in either the right amounts or of the right quality, partly but not entirely, because it does not overcome what have, since Bellerby's day, come to be known as the "free-rider" and "externality" problems.

When Bellerby published A *Contributive Society*, Pigou's *Economics of Welfare* had not appeared. The terms external ities, public goods, free-rider and welfare economics as analytical concepts still awaited development. However, he did not think his prime objective was to make out the case for a better set of economic arrangements for society as a whole— that seemed to him self-evident from the outset—rather, his prime concern was to examine what form such new arrangements should take and to consider how they might be put into effect. In spite of this major difference in aim and emphasis it is illuminating, nevertheless, to trace out the extent to which Bellerby anticipated so many of the elements in modern so-called developed society which Hirsch was, in due course, to analyse so brilliantly. Parallel, usually brief quotations will be employed to identify some of the more important points that feature in both their works.

Social Limits *to Growth and* A Contributive Society: *issues of concern to both*

On positional goods and the problems to which they give rise (*Social Limits*, p. 2), "If everyone stands on tiptoe, no-one sees better"; (*Contributive Society*, p. 47), "Men live in crowds; if some use their elbows, others suffer".

On individual and community behaviour norms (*Social Limits*, p. 147), "Reliance on socialised norms alone—on individuals directing themselves to do what the community expects of them—would be extremely inefficient as well as oppressive . . . the principle of meeting the wants of others can be as alienating as the principle of acting only against fair exchange'. (*Contributive Society*, p. 92), "Satisfying though this 'imaginative other-interest' may be as a motive, it can be of no value independently. It may lead to a large contributiveness; it may produce wider satisfaction; or it may create universal social warmth; but it can achieve these things only in association with its counterpart 'self-interest'. Alone, 'other-interest' would produce a vacuum".

On whether there is a role to be played by central direction of individual behaviour (*Social Limits*, p. 180), "While deliberate action cannot or should not be used directly to legislate and enforce a change in individual motives and behaviour, it can be applied effectively and legitimately to removing obstacles to such change". (*Contributive Society*, pp. 175/6), "If an employer in the Society had a mind to sow ideas amongst his group he would assuredly not expect success from the exercise of financial control but only from the force of the ideas themselves. Ultimately, external compulsion is powerless: movement and change come only from intellectual persuasion".

The motivation of individuals to achieve personal goals has long been a major interest of economists besides which concern with the motivation of individuals to achieve community goals has been greatly neglected. Bellerby and Hirsch had illuminating observations to make on both types of motivation. (*Social Limits*, p. 145) ". . . where individual preferences can be satisfied in sum only or most efficiently through collective action, privately directed behaviour may lose its inherent advantages over collectively oriented behaviour even as a means to satisfy individual preferences themselves, however self-interested". However, Hirsch also expressed doubts about the ability of society to set meaningful limits to individual motivation (*Social Limits*, p. 131), "At the individual or micro-level, therefore, motivation under managed capitalism has to be kept in compartments; but there is no obvious way of communicating to individuals just where maximisation of private interests is to stop short". And (p. 179), "But some mechanism is needed through which the changed social need is transmitted to individual actions. The trouble is that such a mechanism cannot be expected to evolve through the independent responses of individuals". Bellerby is less pessimistic. (*Contributive Society*, p. 142) ". . . the urge to contribute effectively would drive those on whom it settled to the adoption of some form of organisation" and "The condition from which the beginning is made is that each member shall be bent on making the 'maximum contribution' (to the welfare of society)."

On the free-rider problem (*Social Limits*, p. 135), ". . . the rational individualist in situations of social interdependence knows that he does best when everyone *else* co-operates and he does not" (*Contributive Society*, p. 85), "All depends upon the purposes inspiring those who acquire and use . . . property . . . the good and bad in competition are dependent essentially on the motives of the competitors". And (p. 146), "It is self-interest which makes men conceal their gains, refuse to compromise and grasp and retain the limit of what the economic system permits them".

On positional competition (*Social Limits*, p. 176), "Positional competition . . . demolishes conceptual harmony. Inequalities are now more directly connected to what individuals seek; here, one man's gain is another man's loss". (*Contributive Society*, p. 84) "The motive (of self-interest) itself, when carried to an extreme, fails completely to satisfy the accepted test of 'harmony'. By its very nature extreme self-interest involves a struggle amongst individuals to acquire a large share of a limited common fund of goods, to force themselves above others, and to attain liberties which trench upon the liberties of others". Hirsch echoes this on page 20, "A second classification of consumer scarcity is social, consumer demand is concentrated on particular goods and facilities that are limited in actual supply, not by physical but by social factors, including the satisfaction engendered by scarcity as such . . . This social limitation may be derived, most directly and most familiarly, from psychological motives of various kinds, notably envy, emulation or pride. Satisfaction is derived from relative position alone, of being in front, or from others being behind".

On the redistribution of income and wealth (*Social Limits*, p. 140), "In cases like redistribution of income . . . internalised altruistic norms of behaviour would not be a substitute for the necessary central direction of individual actions, although such norms are likely to help implement the necessary collective policy. . .". And again (p. 177), "The internal forces released by liberal capitalism have exerted pressures for conscious justification of economic rewards, a pressure that undermines the system's drive and equipoise. That is the current crisis of the system". (*Contributive Society*, p. 55) "The possibility of securing a redistribution (of ownership and income) through taxation or through profit-ownership sharing schemes is limited by our meagre standards of generosity; the meagreness of these standards being due, again, to the general belief that to retain property is a 'right' ".

It is evident that Hirsch and Bellerby were both concerned about the growth of structural inefficiencies and about unfairness as economies develop. Moreover, they both concentrated their attention largely on similar areas of economic and social activity. However, Hirsch was mostly concerned with working out the implications of his ideas on positional competition and with the inadequacy of traditional economic policies to meet present needs, while Bellerby contrasted the system as he found it, unfair and often poor and shoddy, with what it might achieve if individual motivation could be inspired to seek more worthy and fairer goals. Hirsch's analysis is, throughout, focused primarily on society's problems while Bellerby's is directed, in the main, at reaching answers to those problems, identified in broadly similar terms to those employed by Hirsch. Nevertheless, Hirsch does come to the very far-reaching conclusion that society, in the so-called developed world, cries out for a new moral under-pinning if its increasingly complex social and economic arrangements are not to become increasingly unfair, frustrating and socially wasteful (*Social Limits*, p. 190), "We may be near the limit of explicit social organisation possible without a supporting social morality. Additional correctives in its absence simply do not take. That is the decisive weakness of the purely technocratic approach to keeping the market economy to its social purpose". Although Hirsch did not pursue the implications of that line of thought beyond that point, it is nevertheless a remarkable conclusion for someone to reach who was embarked on a positive study of society's economic and social problems with no particular normative ideals to establish. No less remarkable is the relative lack of attention which that conclusion has produced.

Bellerby's method of working was directed at trying to establish, largely introspectively, what an ideal set of socio-economic arrangements should achieve and, having done so, to put into practice his ideas about how to move society towards such a set of arrangements. He was nothing if not pragmatic and courageous. His approach was at one and the same time practical, operational and idealistic; and seldom far from lyrical. Some key elements of his system are the following.

As a preliminary working arrangement personal expenditure is to be confined to the "average wage", but this is best thought of only as an "external form" adopted so that every individual may make his "maximum contribution" to the whole of society. Wages as such are to be determind as part of the normal competitive market process; those earning less than the average will, therefore, have to be paid a subsidy to bring their spending power up to the average. For the rest all is to be focussed on making everyone's "maximum contribution" possible.

Such a society is seen as coming about as a result of the formation of essentially local groups designed to achieve agreed social capital formation programmes. Indeed (p. 197), "Individuals would only come together on the basis of the desire to pursue some limited common aim". Groups are to be local because only in this way will spending be kept within the controlling influence of the individuals who had had the "travail" of producing that investible surplus. Such groups are envisaged as becoming progressively more numerous as time goes on. But, Bellerby argues, the true gain to society is not simply the social capital that such groups will create, rather, it will be (p. 187) "the psychological advantage which results when members of society find themselves able to pool their possessions". In that way the acquisitive motive will be "put in its place" giving way to "an absence of mental obsession from which a completely sane view of property can be developed". Progress is seen as being (p. 187) "by contagion". All the same, the aims of the group would not be easily arrived at but (p. 150) "would represent the focus, not merely of spare-time or casual interest, but of the entire business and social enterprise of its members . . . something of the nature of an agreed life-philosophy". Such groups would (p. 152) "strive to supplement rather than to overlap the services ordinarily provided by the state or city". Strikingly (p. 160), private property would be retained only where it could be "regarded as a more effective means of attaining certain ends than communal property".

Although Hirsch acknowledges the strength of incentives to achieve group aims, nevertheless the general balance of his views on the subject of co-operation is sceptical. (*Social Limits*, p. 136) "Since co-operation (of this kind) is normally difficult and costly to organise, latent collective interests, particularly of large groups, will not be mobilised by voluntary action unless particular private benefits can be built in as an incentive to participate". Again (p. 145), Hirsch's awareness of the free-rider problem is evident, "Voluntary participation in the provision of a collective good . . . cannot be expected to be induced merely by approval of the specific collective objective. For at the individual level, personal participation is neither sufficient nor necessary to secure the collective objective". Hirsch sees the need for change but does not argue that only by some radical transformation of human nature can it be achieved. Thus (*Social Limits*, p. 189), "More . . . collective provision and collective orientation . . . in turn demand some adjustment in perceptions. What is involved here is not a revolutionary change in attitudes, the visionary 'change in human nature', but an adjustment of degree". Yet *Social Limits* does not leave its reader feeling either that society *will* find the answer it needs nor that Hirsch was ready to put one forward. Bellerby had no such fears; if change for the better was to come it would be through example and local initiative and through education. Best of all it should come from the combination of both, from "Societies" at local level pioneering in the field of education in order to provide the long-term direction and drive of society at large. Bellerby never wanted his reader to lose sight of that (p. 24); "sooner or later a type of education should emerge which will raise the mind to its position of ascendancy over those bodily enslavements which give self-interest its peculiar power". In the meantime it is clear that Bellerby regards a large part of society's ills as stemming from "excessive" self-interest.

However, although he is less specific and forthright on this point than is Hirsch, he does not go so far as to deny (as Hirsch does) that the individual with a "larger view" can, if present in large enough numbers, correct the system.

Indeed, it is from the eventually all pervading motivation to contribute that Bellerby envisages all else must follow. The free-rider problem will not arise. Externalities will disappear in the face of an abhorrence of the shoddy and sordid on the one hand and zoned development of certain sectors of industry on the other. (*Contributive Society*, p. 151) "an attack on unsightliness . . . the clearing of slums; the protection of open spaces; the abolition of factors of dirt, smoke, noise, disease: the preservation of rural beauty". Industrial relations will be transformed in the process of creating a generalised system of co-ownership (pp. 209/210), "The generalisation of the Society's principles relating to property and ownership would produce a situation in which almost all persons would have the double function of employer and employee". . . . "industry would be composed of a vast number of teams, each member of a team having a double role".

Chapter VI is devoted to setting out the stages by which society is to be expected to progress towards its ideal state. Two ideas are paramount, first, average consumption, or something near it; second, spending the surplus so released for the agreed, *locally relevant*, good of society at large. Moreover, it has to be stressed that that *is* the way Bellerby saw it. He did not argue for a widespread movement towards greater equality of personal spending through taxation so as to permit greater state spending on Government identified projects. Nor did he argue for the fiscal encouragement of trusts and charities aimed at providing the community with public and near public goods. It is not that he would not have approved of such ventures, indeed we know they enjoyed his support and encouragement, rather it is that for him they would have failed to aim high enough. His groups had to face the question (p. 150) "what do we desire for *man*?" The approach employed is a mixture of the practical and the idealistic. Some will conclude, perhaps over-hastily, that it suffers on that account. It is helpful, therefore, to compare Bellerby's approach to the problem of achieving a more just set of economic arrangements in society with the attempt by Rawls in his book, *Economic Justice*, to specify, uniquely and incontrovertibly, the logical foundations on which such a set of arrangements can be erected.

A Contributive Society *and* Economic Justice

Bellerby's aim for society is clear from the outset (p. x) "Assume the existence of a community of individuals who satisfy the most exacting definition of social merit, and then ask the question: How would they act? What principles would they set up to govern their economic conduct? . . . Perfection in this respect, expressed in economic terms, would consist in 'the desire to make the maximum contribution to communal consumption' ".

Bellerby's approach is, therefore, in marked contrast to that of John Rawls as set out in his pioneering study, *A Theory of Justice,* Harvard University Press (1971), where it is argued that a principle of distributive justice will never be reached so long as people think about it from the socio-economic positions they already occupy in life. Instead, they should divorce themselves from those positions and imagine they do not know how they might fare in the natural lottery of life. Various phrases bring out Rawls's intention—there is to be a 'veil of ignorance' separating everyone in the original bargaining position from his actual lot in life. It is to be "as if one's born enemy" is allocating one's talents and resources. The supposition is crucial for on it is based the next and fundamental step which is to argue that the fear of being worst off in life's natural lottery will be paramount so that everyone will agree that economic affairs must be so regulated as to maximise the long-term, lifetime, prospects of the most disadvantaged. Rawls is concerned to *derive* this conclusion and so establish its unique, logical status. His arguments run roughly as follows:

(i) In the "original" or "contractual" position in which the appropriate ethical principle is to be selected, certain needs will possess "infinite" marginal utility and, therefore, call to be served before all else. Those needs are variously described but, at this stage, can be summarised as political liberty, the primary material needs of life and education. Thus[1] ". . . given

[1] The quotations are from John Rawls's article, 'Distributive Justice', printed in *Economic Justice*, pp. 319–62, Penguin Modern Economics Readings, 1973, edited by E. S. Phelps.

the complete lack of knowledge (which makes the choice one under uncertainty) the fact that the decision involves one's life prospects as a whole and is constrained by strict obligations to third parties (e.g. one's descendants) and duties to certain values (e.g. to religious truth), it is rational to be conservative and so to choose in accordance with an analogue of the maximin principle. . . . since we must guarantee our personal and spiritual liberties, 'marginal utility' is infinite and this leads to greater risk aversion and so to maximise, at least with respect to these liberties".

(ii) The *inevitability* of this conclusion (frequently referred to as the second or difference principle) is reinforced by the notion of rationality which Rawls employs; ". . . it is rational for a person to choose as if he were designing a society in which his enemy is to assign him his place". And "I shall assume that expectations are specified by the expected pattern of primary goods, that is, things which rational persons may be presumed to want whatever else they want . . ." . . . "among the primary goods are liberty and opportunity, income and wealth, health and educated intelligence. Perhaps the most important is self-respect; a confident conviction of the sense of one's own value, a firm assurance that what one does and plans to do is worth doing".

Further, "expectation is a function of the whole institutional structure: it can be raised and lowered by reassigning rights and duties throughout the system. Thus the expectation of any position depends upon the expectations of the others, and these in turn depend upon the pattern of rights and duties established by the basic structure". Critically, and especially with regard to inheritance, "something will be allowable . . . if and only if the greater expectations of the more advantaged when playing a part in the working of the whole social system

improves the expectations of the least advantaged . . .".
Thus, ". . . no one gains (or loses) from his luck in the natural
lottery of talent and ability, or from his initial place in society,
without giving (or receiving) compensatory advantages in
return". Equally critically, when questions of what is and what
is not to be allowed are raised, "Let us suppose that
inequalities are chain connected: that is, if an inequality raises
the expectations of the lower position, it raises the expectations of all positions in between".

The first principle according to which equality of basic liberties applies compatible with a similar scheme of liberties for all
is not in contention; it not only embodies a test of generality of
treatment, but is crucial in drawing up rules for the furtherance of competition in an economy. However, while everyone
has praised Rawls's vision and analytical approach, they are by
no means agreed that the second or "difference" principle has
been established as an incontestable expression of distributive
justice. If the ignorance of society's members in the design
stage of the social contract really were complete (as Rawls
requires), can it be demonstrated that the maximin criterion
would inevitably result in the difference principle being formu-
lated? Would it by dint of that ignorance thereby achieve universal moral applicability and lose every vestige of
contingency?

Although critics have not accepted the difference principle
as universally compelling, it can be argued that this is because
they have never divorced themselves completely from their
real-life socio-economic rankings, and that this failure is borne
out in their unwillingness to accept the asymmetrical pattern
of sacrifice the principle imposes on the more talented and better endowed. However, ignorance of one's own position in
society does not extend to not knowing what *general* socio-
economic groupings characterise society. And, since it does

not, what is to be said in reply to the individual who, knowing the odds on coming out in one group or another, says, nevertheless, that he will take his chance? Is he to be branded as immoral because of it? He might argue that, to be human is to be unequal; life is a lottery; the rule of the lottery is to make the most of life and accept whatever turns out. That sort of attitude would not necessarily run counter to the view that no-one deserves to inherit wealth or talent while at the same time recognising that, to go on to look for a compensation principle for the disadvantaged, is to go beyond that thought. Some do not take that further step on moral or humanitarian grounds although they might, for example, on grounds of fear. Some go beyond that first thought but not so far as the difference principle.

Rawls's answer to such faltering is that no right-thinking person can fail to see that the difference principle is just; right-thinking persons identify with the misfortunes, hopes and aspirations of their fellows. Rational people need to feel they earn their material well-being and good fortune. Now, however, the difference principle derives from the notion of rational and the process is to this extent tautological. In the end, Rawls seems not unaware that he is not in the world of ultimates, but is pleading and persuading, not demonstrating, for he writes, "The main question is perhaps whether he is prepared to accept the further definition of one's conception of right which the two principles represent".

This seems of little importance. The fact that society is unfair calls for some measure of correction. To respond for base motives would be unworthy. It is necessary that some notion of what is right should be brought to bear on the issue. However, society need scarcely feel compelled to await the demonstration that some completely unchallengeable principle is available.

Rawls clearly attaches great importance to the systematic and desirable resource allocation outcomes which result from the interplay of what are essentially selfishly inspired, personal motives and actions, aimed at securing one's own gain. However, although he clearly favours a system in which individuals are free to order their own affairs wherever possible, he does not explore in depth how maximising rewards to the worse-off would operate except that, their rewards would take the form of earnings (rewards for their own efforts), transfers from the rest of society to them as individuals belonging to the class of its least fortunate members and public goods which would be available for all, but would have been designed very much with their needs in mind; nevertheless, transfers would not increase without limit because to do so would reduce donor incentives and effort so that gains to the poor from transfers out of taxes would eventually be offset by corresponding losses from reduced earnings to bear those transfers. However, it is surely heroic to claim that a benign interconnectedness or chain linking of events exists, not only between a permitted receipt of benefit by some members of society's more advantaged classes and the more disadvantaged in society, but that everyone in intermediary locations as well benefits proportionately.

Although not relying on such macro-economic heroics, Bellerby leaves a lot to the growth of fellow-feeling and the wish to make maximum social contribution; in so doing he stands to achieve more as a result of reduced externalities, fewer free-riders and improved industrial relations. His approach is expansive, generous and visionary. However, some will swiftly translate his initial thoughts into the cynical escapist observation that "people get the socio-economic system that they deserve". Others will regard as naïve, ingenuous and tautological claims like (*Contributive Society,*

p. 37) "Any feature which lends harmony to the system must possess intrinsically the power to satisfy the majority working within the system. Further, a factor which increases harmony must thereby reinforce all tendencies towards co-operation and raise the efficiency of the system, so that, whatever may be the aims to be attained through it they will be secured most effectively".

Many will doubt the power of social goals to call forth sufficient intensity of effort and singleness of purpose when individual rewards are limited to the "average wage". On page 186, "The amount to be pooled (i.e. transferred to the Society) would be left to the discretion of each individual". But would that not let in the free-rider? (Page 60) "The right of inheritance would, it seems, almost certainly be abolished". However (p. 189), to accept the principle of corporate ownership ". . . would not signify that no provision would be made for sons and heirs". Even the impressive attack on equality as any final and proper goal of social endeavour will be hailed by some as the Achilles heel of the system that will bring all to nought. Nothing less than a full quotation can do it justice however. (*Contributive Society*, p. 214) "Aesthetically, equality is a thing to loathe . . . A regime which ruled all to a common average would strike much from life, both in its physical and spiritual expression, first limiting possessions, then, through them indirectly, limiting people. For it would begin by causing all to frame their physical life to a confined pattern; to build their homes much to pattern; to dress, furnish, take their pleasure and make their meals to pattern. Then, conformity in deeds would inevitably bring in its train conformity in spirit. When the non-conforming mind is deprived of an outlet, it must in the course of time lose strength. Conventions emerge and check spontaneity, each individual being held and circumscribed and trimmed by his social circle. Society stiffens, and sinks, if averaging is the rule, to a dull level of mediocrity".

It is hard to charge Bellerby with paying insufficient attention to practical issues for his book abounds with penetrating and policy relevant observations. Some are amazingly far-sighted. Space allows only one or two quotations.

On War (p. 23), "Up to the present the surplus powers of nations, instead of being applied to development that is constructive and educative, have to a large extent been squandered in wars, . . . various 'plausible ideals' woven around semi-virtuous sentiments such as empire have held the thoughts of educators, . . . Only when there is no more war and no more fear of war will these ideals begin to fade and others take their place. This stage cannot be so many decades distant, it would seem, if for no other reason than that progress in the science of slaying in the long run itself militates against war."

On teaching Religion (p. 114), "The essence of the finding in this case must be that the nature of the educational system is of no significance whatever; it can make little difference whether the religion is formally included or not; for if the teacher has no religion he will convey nothing, except a little history, even though the subject be included; if he has religion it will escape from him and have its effect with or without the actual lesson".

On Communism (p. 33), "No change in structure of the economic system should be attempted which goes *radically* beyond the powers of human character . . . (p. 34). Communism which was the regime at first attempted is essentially a spiritual ideal, and could only be made effective through universal altruism. To attempt to force it on a people at the point of the sword as was done, initially, is the most cynical form of contradiction".

On Nationalisation (p. 164), "The industries which are most suitable for nationalisation are those which provide essential public services; tend ordinarily towards monopoly (e.g. are subject to the law of increasing returns); involve no great risk; yield services or goods which admit of standardisation in quality; have a stereotyped form of administration; raise no serious problem of discipline; do not throw Governments of different countries into economic conflict with one another; and lend themselves to arbitrary price-fixing and wage-fixing".

In Conclusion

At each and every stage of the arguments assembled in *A Contributive Society* is Bellerby's vision of the economic system as a set of human relationships (p. 35,) "This is not a prophecy, but merely the statement of a law. When the economic system is seen exactly as it is—a complex of human 'habits' every one of which has come into existence under the pressure of human motives, has been shaped by human minds, and has been adapted to meet both the strength and weakness of human character—the conclusion directly follows that to change the economic system is to change human character, and *vice versa*". And he never retreats from that position when faced with the most "practical" of issues. However, between that view of society and Hirsch there lies a chasm which the latter found quite unbridgeable (*Social Limits*, p. 139), "Christianity sets great store by altruistic behaviour. The point emphasised here is that if this is undertaken as a means to religious ends, it also acts as a means to functionally necessary social cooperation for individualistic earthly ends. In this function, it is the altruistic behaviour that counts and not what motives happen to underlie it—whether Christian values, social pressure, conformist, cowardice, humanitarianism, or anything else". Bellerby would have considered that plain fare indeed, though with his customary generosity and broadness of outlook he would have acknowledged, regrettably, its core of truth.

Yet, perhaps the most serious obstacle of all to progress towards a more just society has nowhere been expressed better than by Hirsch (p. 155), "No unqualified distinction can be made between restraint of economic power that is explicitly exerted in some political or organisational form and direct economic power that flows from market opportunities. Rather, restraint over politically organised economic power, which is likely to take the form of disruptive power, has to be considered in the context of what restraint, if any, is exercised on independent acquisitive power in the sense of market opportunities". It is, we know, a feature of society that Bellerby was familiar enough with at first hand in the 1930s. Things have scarcely improved since those days but, if the tripartite answer of *A Contributive Society*, fairer remuneration, better industrial relations through participation in decision making and more of society's "surplus" going to create social capital, is not acceptable, what is?

Bellerby's vision of society admits, in the final analysis, of no paraphrase and he must be allowed to speak for himself (p. 216), . . . "Once the base of the social structure had been made sound, a society bent on contribution would collect itself for an intense effort to escape from deadening monotony. It would concentrate on building upwards, in spires, from the solid base. In such an attempt there would be two main forms of building: that which implies corporate expression; and that which implies individual expression. In both cases, variety, and grandeur, and scope would seem indispensable to achievement . . .'. And (p. 220) "Although equality must rank high as an initial aim, being the inevitable outcome of that sympathy which gives society its meaning, yet there is beyond and above and almost absorbing it a further aim, which we may call the Higher Beauty. By this is meant the art of expression of the whole body of the people viewed as a harmony . . . it is this in the service of which each may acquire freedom, partly because its service means full outreaching, partly because it implies unison and not conflict with other effort".

A CONTRIBUTIVE SOCIETY

BY

J. R. BELLERBY

REVIEW

BY

P. A. SLOAN

The Economic Journal
VOL CXII No 4570. March 1931

"THERE appear to be two chief difficulties confronting those who are anxious to see some change in the 'economic system.' The first is that of visualising a system which would in all ways reflect or express their ideal; the second is that of determining what steps may be taken, here and now, towards the attainment of the ideal" (p. vii). In this book Professor Bellerby analyses the imperfections of the existing economic system, expresses in general terms what he considers to be the conditions essential to an ideal system, and then attempts to answer the difficult question: "How far is it possible, immediately, to press forward towards the ideal?" (p. xi). It is in answering this question that Professor Bellerby differs most fundamentally from the Marxists, for, in so far as the ideal is concerned, he has much in common with them. The Marxian ideal of a State in which each contributes according to his ability and receives according to his needs is very close indeed to Professor Bellerby's ideal of "a community of men whose accepted aim was to contribute their maximum to the consumption of the entire group" (p. xi). But while the Marxists maintain that the transition from the present state of society to the ideal must take place primarily through a change in institutions, thus causing the contributive spirit to develop as a consequence, Professor Bellerby envisages a transition in which individuals must develop the contributive spirit and thus alter institutions. He considers that "undoubtedly, certain methods of social reconstruction, the legislative and the educational, do make for the greatest possible width of advance; but the advance is correspondingly narrow in depth. . . . There is, however, a second possible way of advance. It consists in the establishment of small pockets of society, groups which are bent on making personal experiment towards some social model" (p. xii). It is this method which appears to the author to be most consistent with the ideal before him.

"For some reason, not readily understood, the question of the underlying driving force of industry appears to have been largely omitted from the sphere of 'economics.' The tendency has been to regard this subject as falling within the scope of ethics." But "sooner or later the economist or social leader who recommends new economic mechanism without reference to the power available to drive it will come to be judged as, say, an engineer who builds machinery for which no suitable form of power can be found" (p. 5). We may see the point of this statement of the author if we ask, for example, how far the orthodox criticisms of socialism are only justified on the assumption that human motive in the economic life of a socialist community will be no different from the motive underlying the economic life of an individualist society. The assumption of orthodox economists, that self-interest is the prime mover of all individuals, while true to some extent in the economic life of an individualist community, might no longer be true in a community based on different principles from those commonly accepted to-day. Professor Bellerby readily admits that "the grip of self-interest . . . is exceedingly tenacious; for its foundations are laid in a series of ever-present and compelling bodily cravings. . . . It does not necessarily follow, however, that because self-interest has a psychological basis which is permanent, it will always be dominant" (p. 22). It may be quite impossible for many of us to believe that individuals can ever be prompted in their lives by any motive, ultimately, other than the desire for satisfaction through self-expression; but this does not imply that self-expression cannot take other forms than the personal accumulation of wealth; it may take the form of making the maximum contribution to general welfare if this activity is believed to be worth more than mere acquisition. The business man who has "made his pile" rarely retires from business. Not because his material needs are not yet satisfied, but because in order to feel that he is a satisfactory member of society he must be accumulating wealth. If the measure of satisfactoriness were the amount contributed and not the amount acquired, the motive governing production might alter in a very short time, as has doubtlessly occurred to a considerable extent in Russia. In finding the root of the evils of the present economic system in human motive the author challenges the most fundamental assumption of orthodox economics. He puts a very strong case for a reconsideration of the value of this assumption if we visualise society as a changing organism in every way, and not as one in which the most anti-social of human characteristics cannot change.

We now come to the principles to be put into effect by those who, in society as it exists to-day, accept the ideal of "maximum contribution" and desire to bring into existence a community in which this is the ruling motive of human action.

"Since it is to the community as a whole that the gift is to be made, the contributor necessarily ranks himself equally with all others for benefits; and he attempts to assess his share by making some estimate of the 'average wage.' The attempt to limit consumption to this average, whilst following naturally upon any contributive urge, might nevertheless in some cases, by its reaction of the individual, reduce his power to serve; and in such cases 'maximum contribution' would involve consumption greater than the average" (p. 139). In making this concession it may appear that Professor Bellerby is admitting the validity of the excuse which has been given for every act of exploitation that has ever been perpetrated, but it may be replied that if the aim of the individual is maximum contribution, then he never will increase his consumption beyond the point at which he believes it will help him. The question is, will his belief be affected by his desires? and this question cannot be answered with certainty. Some doubt may also be felt as to the "average wage" basis of income. Why not make it average income, for example, in which case the personal income is only the material sign of a change of motive; if the motive has really changed there is no doubt that the individual will limit his consumption to a minimum, whereas if the motive has not really been altered, then, to whatever extent he limits his income, he will, in fact, be able to gain more than the average material satisfaction by various subversive means. It appears that too much stress should not be laid on the actual material limitations which Professor Bellerby suggests.

Given that a Society of individuals accepting the principle of maximum contribution and the average wage has been formed, what kind of work are they to undertake in an acquisitive community? In answering this question it is suggested that they should take part in ordinary economic life, with certain limitations. "If any member were an architect, or a teacher, or a welfare worker, or a manufacturer of artistic wares, he would be contributing directly to the stated aims of the Society. Another method would be through deriving funds from work in industry and devoting them to the 'common purposes' " (p. 153) of the Society. "Property should be held in such a way that it would yield most benefit, present and future. During early life much might be held in private hands, so that it might be transferred readily from use to use" (p. 193). Inheritance would be eliminated, but the Society would provide insurances for its members. In industrial activity socially-harmful trades would be avoided, competition as a means to fostering enterprise and ability would be utilised, but would give way to co-operation wherever it proved unsatisfactory. "In industrial relations the attempt" would be made "to arrive at a position in which all persons share the ownership of, and the responsibility for, industry; and the creation of an attitude to production such that every business unit, as a body, becomes a public service" (p. 194) would be fostered. The question, to what extent the Society would be justified in benefiting from the profits gained by individual members, is unfortunately not discussed. The conflict which might arise between the duty of a member to the Society whose only aim was to maximise its contribution to the community in the long run, and his obligation direct to the community through his work, appears hardly to have been considered, though the solution of this problem is essential to any satisfactory working of the Society. For example, if the Society were greatly in need of funds for important social work, would its members be justified in raising the prices of their services to the community in order that these funds be obtained, or would this constitute an unjustifiable exploitation of the community for the benefit of the Society? Societies of this kind have existed in the past in isolation, so that the methods of the acquisitive world could be completely renounced. In bringing his Society into close contact with economic life, Professor Bellerby certainly increases its power to influence that life, but the need for compromises with the desire for acquisition is at the same time substantially increased.

The Society could, as it grew, split up into self-governing units, distributed throughout the acquisitive community, in the form of "numerous separate, independent trusts, organised either on an industrial or on a social basis" (p. 197). These organisations would act as an example to other producing organisations and would recruit new members as their success became apparent. By degrees these larger units would be found to affect the State itself, though this stage of development is unfortunately very slightly considered by the author. He maintains that, "irrespective of the stage of growth reached in economic matters, there will still be a necessity for State organisation, law, and government, of much the same kind as that which exists now, so long as any form of disregard or carelessness prevails. . . . It follows, therefore, that the Contributive Society's organisation could never completely supplant that of the State" (p. 212). Unfortunately, the relationship which would exist between two powerful bodies of this kind is not discussed, except in so far as it is suggested that the branches of the Society would be law-abiding, tax-paying institutions. It may be doubted whether the Society and the State would not in fact become identical when the mass of the population had become members of the Society, for by then the community as a whole would have accepted the "contributive" principle and the maintaining of law and order would be no more than a process of administration.

Throughout the book the author has the needs of the individual at heart and deals interestingly with problems and experiments in education, the nature of self-interest, personality, the encouragement of artistic expression, and the danger of the desire for power as a substitute for the acquisitive motive. He covers a field far wider than that which is normally treated by orthodox economics. In considering the position of Russia he states the fundamental difference between himself and the Marxists in the following words: "To attempt to force it (Communism) on a people at the point of the sword, as was done initially, is the most cynical form of contradiction" (p. 34). It may be asked here whether some compromise is not necessary between the two methods of attaining to the ideal society. While the contributive spirit is undoubtedly essential, is it not probably also essential that anti-social minorities should be compelled to conform to any widespread movement? And can it not be said that the Russian revolution was, in fact, a rather bloody instance of such coercion? The part to be played by Professor Bellerby's Society in the community of the future seems very analogous to the activity of the Communist Party in Russia to-day, with one difference, that the Communists do not restrict themselves only to conversion by example. In both cases we have what may be called "economic asceticism, " that phenomenon which shows signs of spreading and bringing about the one change in "human nature" which has hitherto been considered by the mass of people to be impossible. It will be interesting to see to what extent the contributive society of the future will be indebted to the economic asceticism of the persuasive variety, and to what extent to the economic asceticism of the Communists, and to what extent a compromise between the two may be effected.

This book challenges the existing economic system, and finds strength in its sincerity. It should be inspiring to all those who have not been hardened by too long an acquaintance with the orthodox conception of human nature. Professor Bellerby is fair-minded, perhaps too fair-minded to have the maximum propaganda value, for he is acutely conscious of the problems with which his thesis confronts both us and him. For this reason, in certain places, an extreme broad-mindedness may give the impression of a lack of faith in the proposals made; which is a pity. Ultimately, Professor Bellerby is more than an economist, he is an artist in the widest sense of the term, and is aiming at an ideal far wider than anything which can be expressed in the limited terminology of economics. This ultimate ideal he calls the "Higher Beauty. By this is meant the art of expression of the whole body of the people, viewed as a harmony; a thing of infinite variety combined into one vast life symphony. It is the counterpart in man's activity of that of Nature, where infinitesimals and infinites contrast, and where nothing is so small as to be neglected and nothing so great as to overbear the whole. It is this human Higher Beauty that demands the contribution of each artist; and it is this in the service of which each may acquire freedom, partly because its service means full outreaching, partly because it implies unity and not conflict with other effort" (p. 221).

University College,
Bangor.

POSTSCRIPT

Major J. R. Bellerby

[Ray Manning, doing what we all frequently plan to do but seldom achieve, was cleaning out an accumulation of old papers when he came across a cutting from *The Times* of 5 April 1977. It was an obituary of Major Bellerby, which, among other things, said: ". . . Returning (from World War I in which he served with distinction) to Leeds University, he took a brilliant First and was appointed to the staff of the International Labour Offfice in Geneva, then its great days as a centre on labour problems."

I asked Archie Evans if he remembered Bellerby, and Archie replied:]

Yes, I did know him quite well. It is largely due to him that I joined the staff of the ILO. He was my "Director of Studies" at Cambridge during the latter part of my studies there. He had, as the obituary notice you sent me pointed out, previously been in the ILO. I think he had been working on, at this end, a report on unemployment in the coalmining industry, a problem which is still with us.

In my post-graduate year, Bellerby was conducting a special round table at the joint request of the Brunner-Mond group of employers and of the Trades Union Congress on the consequences of the return to the gold standard by Britain, and the effects of monetary policy on employment.

At that time, the League of Nations was just about to appoint the Gold Delegation of the Financial Committee, which was to discuss the impact of the purchasing power of gold on the economic life of the nations. The ILO wanted the impact of the monetary situation on employment and on real wages to be fully taken into account, and not purely monetary and financial matters. Robert Fuss, Chief of the Unemployment and Migration Section, was the ILO observer at the Gold Delegation, and I was appointed to his service largely because of my Cambridge activities, which had been reported on by Bellerby to the ILO. It was my job to prepare briefs for Fuss and to sit in on the Gold Delegation. There were other "juniors" there, who very often disagreed with their chiefs and rewrote bits of the reports as they would have liked to see them. Some of them rose to good positions later.

Bellerby later wrote a very challenging book called *The Contributive Society* (London, Education Services, 1931) which really meant an idealistic economic society in which people's motivation was to maximise their contribution to the welfare of society rather than to draw as much out of the system as possible for themselves. Some of us international officials have perhaps been unconsciously inspired by this approach. One of his followers in this field, who tried to live in accordance with these principles for a time in spite of inheriting a title and a good deal of money, was Lord Listowel, Viscount Ennismore, who was, when I was up for a term, President of the Union Society in Cambridge (the main debating society). The difficulties encountered by Bellerby led him to publish in 1933 *The Conflict of Values* (London, Richard Clay & Son). Ennismore, for his part, published *The Values of Life* (London, George Allen & Unwin, 1931) in which he discusses the problem of trying to live under Bellerby's principles. The book, a short one, is dedicated to Jack Bellerby.

These volumes are still, today, on my shelf of "Utopias".

As for what Bellerby did during his relatively short spell at the ILO, it would be necessary to look at the Office records, if preserved.*

Bellerby was certainly a most remarkable character, trying to put ethical principles into practice in a wealth-seeking world.

Archie Evans

Bulletin des anciens. I.L.O. Friends Newsletter
No. 5, Geneva, 1 May 1988

---

* An indication of J. R. Bellerby's work during this period is given by his publications, 1923–27, listed in Appendix II.

APPENDIX I

Publications assisted by Education Services since 1974 include:

1988 *The Nature and Significance of Natural Resources in Relation to Human Development. J. O. Jones, in Human Ecology Research and Applications. Society of Human Ecology, Maryland, U.S.A.
       *Pictorial Charts Educational Trust: Catalogue.

1987 *Peace Studies. The Hard Questions. Ed: Elaine Kaye. Oxford Project for Peace Studies.
       *Believing in the Environment. Martin Palmer. Council for Environmental Studies.

1986 *A New Thing. The Story of Daily Bread Cooperative, 1975–85. J. Wallace. Daily Bread Cooperative Ltd. Northampton.
       *Blueprint for 50 Cooperatives. R. Sawtell. Cooperative Development Agency.
       *Law and Human Ecology in the Commonwealth. Volume 2. The Gambia: Water Supply and Control. A. J. Adamson, B. H. Barrett, H. K. Heer, R. W. L. Howells, J. O. Jones. Commonwealth Secretariat.

1984 An Economic Analysis of the Introduction of Legislation governing the Welfare of Farm Animals. Frances Sandiford. Faculty of Economic and Social Studies, University of Manchester.

1985 A Peaceful Economy? Defence Conversion and the Arms Industry in the U.S.A. Tom Woodhouse. School of Peace Studies, University of Bradford.
       *Law and Human Ecology in the Commonwealth. Volume 1. Ghana: Water Supply and Control. A. J. Adamson, B. H.

Barrett, H. K. Heer, R. W. L. Howells, J. O. Jones. Commonwealth Secretariat.

1983   *Agricultural Commodity Trade in a Regime of Floating Exchange Rates.* K. P. Parris and G. H. Peters. Commonwealth Bureau of Agricultural Economics.

1978   **Organic Farming: Economic, Social and Technical Aspects.* B. Hirst. Commonwealth Human Ecology Council.

1977   **Energy Use in Agriculture (fossil fuels).* B. Hirst. Commonwealth Human Ecology Council.

1974   **Index of Human Ecology.* J. O. Jones and E. A.Jones. Europa Publications.

[Publications by J. R. Bellerby are listed in Appendix II]

Assisted Charities, 1986–1988

Regular grants

*Commonwealth Human Ecology Council.
*World Education Fellowship (including biennial book prize)

Contact payments in token of earlier members' interests and involvement

Braziers Adult College
The Caldicott Community
Caius House, Battersea
Invalid Children's Aid Association
Methodist International House
National Society for Cancer Relief
Quaker International Centre
Quaker Peace and Service
Royal Society for Nature Conservation
Society for the Protection of Animals in North Africa
Universities Federation for Animal Welfare

Grants to educational institutions and for youth training and experimental work (some recurring)

Association for Curriculum Development
Maranatha Ministries

*Pictorial Charts Educational Trust
Scoraig Teaching Group
Oxford County Education Committee
Advisory Centre for Education
St. Loye's College
Association for all speech-impaired children
E. Adams and Tyrell Burgess: Teachers' Own Records Project
Cold Comfort Farms Trust
North London Rescue Commando
Forest School Camps
International Boys' Town Trust
The Newington Detached Youth Work Project
Bath Industrial History Trust
St. James' Trust: Farm Cooperation in Zambia
Council for Environmental Education
British Trust for Conservation Volunteers
London Wild Life Institution
World Wildlife Fund
The Athene Trust
Ecological Resource Centre
The Soil Association
Henry Doubleday Research Association
*Law and Human Ecology Project
British Veterinary Association Animal Welfare Foundation
Cambridge School of Veterinary Medicine
Medical Educational Trust
Springhill Cancer Rehabilitation Centre
*Oxford Project for Peace Studies
School of Peace Studies, University of Bradford

*Fellowship and Grant for Research into Monetary Theory and the
Practice of Banking*

David C. Price: J. R. Bellerby Senior Research Fellowship, Agricultural Economics Unit, Oxford University
Traidcraft Exchange: feasibility study in banking for the Third World

Grants to individual students, 1986–88

Twelve students were assisted during this period.

*Indicates direct involvement of Education Services member.

APPENDIX II

Publications by J. R. Bellerby include:

1923   "The Controlling Factor in Trade Cycles". *Economic Journal*, Vol. xxxiii, Sept.

1924   "The Monetary Policy of the Future". *Economic Journal*, Vol. xxxiv, June.
Control of Credit as a Remedy for Unemployment. P. S. King.
The Regularization of Industry. Christian Order of Industry Services.

1925   *Stabilization of Employment in the United States*. International Labour Office.
Monetary Stability. Macmillan & Co. Ltd.
"Some International Aspects of Monetary Policy". *American Economic Review*. Vol. xv, No. 1..

1926   Evidence on the *Strong Bill* (Stabilization of Prices), given to the Currency and Banking Committee of the House of Representatives (U.S.A.) HR 7895.

1927   "The evolution of a Wage Adjustment System". *International Labour Review*. Vol. xvi. Nos. 1, 2, 3.
Coal Mining: A European Remedy. Macmillan & Co. Ltd.

1928   *The Need for a Monetary Policy*. Marshall Society.

1929   *The Neighbours Ltd*. Political Economy Club, Cambridge.

1930   "Wages Policy and the Gold Standard in Great Britain" (with K. S. Isles) *International Labour Review*. Vol. xxii, No. 2.

1931   *A Contributive Society*. Education Services.
Presentation to Macmillan Committee on Finance and Industry (Oral Evidence).

1932 "Industrial Survey of Merseyside" (with Caradog Jones).
"World Inflation", republished in *Essays in the Economics of Socialism and Capitalism.* Ed. R. L. Smyth. British Association.

1933 *The Individual and the State.* (address in Liverpool Cathedral).
World Order without Arms. Education Services.
The Conflict of Values. Education Services.

1940 *Post-war Poverty and Unemployment can be prevented,* by Caradog Jones, includes a contribution by J. R. Bellerby.

1943 *Economic Reconstruction.* Macmillan & Co. Ltd.

1945 *Full Employment and State Control,* by Caradog Jones, includes a contribution by J. R. Bellerby.

1952 "Comparison of Skill, Endurance and Experience required in Agriculture and Industry. *Farm Economist.* Vol. VII, No. I.

1953 "U.K.: Comparison of Urban and Rural Retail Prices". *Journal of the Royal Statistical Society.* Vol. cxvi, Pt. 1.
"Farm Incentive Income". *Farm Economist,* Vol. VII, No. 5.
"Farm Occupiers' Capital in the U.K. before 1939". *Farm Economist,* Vol. VII, No. 6.

1954 "Index of Farm Occupiers' Capital in the U.K." (with F. D. W. Taylor) *Farm Economist,* Vol. VII, No. 7.
"Some Causes of the Disparities between Farm and Non-farm Income per head". *Farm Economist,* Vol. VII, No. 8.

1955 "Agricultural Income". *Journal of the Royal Statistical Society.* Vol. cxviii. Pt. 3.
"The Relative Incidence on Agriculturalists and Other Groups of the Benefits resulting from Technical Change". *Proceedings of the International Conference of Agricultural Economists.*
"Marginal Cost Curves in Agriculture". *Farm Economist,* Vol. VIII, No. 1.
"Farm and Non-farm Capital 1867-1938". *Farm Economist,* Vol. VIII, No. 3.

1956 *Agriculture and Industry: Relative Income.* (with others) Macmillan & Co. Ltd.

1958 "Distribution of Manpower in Agriculture and Industry 1851–1951". *Farm Economist*, Vol. IX, No. 1.

1959 "National and Agricultural Income 1851". *Economic Journal*, Vol. LXIX, March.
"Land Maintenance Enquiry". (with J. M. Dunne) *Farm Economist*, Vol. IX, No. 7.
"International Conditions affecting Farm Income Policy". *Farm Economist*, Vol. IX, No. 8.

1960 "Causes of Exceptional Expenditure on Land Maintenance". (with J. M. Dunne) *Farm Economist*, Vol. IX, No. 8.
"Net Return to Farm Land". *Farm Economist*, Vol. IX, No. 8.

1961 *Agricultural Economic Theory and the Indian Economy.* (with N. A. Mujumdar) Vora.

1965 *Farm Animal Welfare and World Food.* (evidence presented to the Bramwell Committee). One World Publication.

1970 *Factory Farming.* (Editor and Contributor). A Symposium edited by J. R. Bellerby on behalf of the British Association for the Advancement of Science, with Foreword by H.R.H. The Prince Philip, Duke of Edinburgh.

1972 *Human Ecology and Human Values* (with M. Allaby and J. O. Jones) U.N. Conference, Stockholm.

1975 *Britain in Debt?* P.S. Authors.